Learning About Peoples and Cultures

PEOPLES AND CULTURES SERIES

Learning About Peoples and Cultures

SEYMOUR FERSH
EDITOR

McDougal, Littell & Company

Evanston, Illinois

New York   Dallas   Sacramento   Raleigh

SEYMOUR FERSH is Professor of Humanities at Brevard Community College, Cocoa, Florida. He has served as Education Director of The Asia Society and as Director of International Services for the American Association of Community and Junior Colleges. Dr. Fersh is also the author of *Asia: Teaching About/Learning From, India and South Asia,* and *The Story of India.*

COVER

The artist on the cover, a woman of the Hmong culture of northern Laos, is stitching an elaborately appliquéd tapestry. Through this creative process, she is enriching not only her own culture but humankind as well. Her individual contribution reminds us of our rich human inheritance. In art such as hers we can celebrate all peoples and cultures. © FPG International Corporation.

BACK COVER

Traditional folk art represents the eight world areas in the *Peoples and Cultures Series.* Clockwise from the upper left: traditional Chinese symbol for happiness and longevity; fantastic bird motif from Latin America; royal elephant from an Indian wall hanging; Japanese crane motif; Islamic geometric design from the Middle East; Hmong pa ndau stitchery motif from Southeast Asia; decorated Ukrainian Easter egg (from *Ukrainian Easter Eggs* by A. Kmit, L. Luciow, J. Luciow, and L. Perchyshyn) from the Soviet Union; carved wood panel from Africa. The world map in the center, courtesy of Maryland CartoGraphics, Inc., symbolizes *Learning About Peoples and Cultures.* Inside the text and *Guide for Teachers, Learning About Peoples and Cultures* will also use another symbol— a human-encircled globe.

Acknowledgments: See page 120

ISBN 0-8123-5791-4

Copyright © 1989 by McDougal, Littell & Company
Box 1667, Evanston, Illinois 60204

15 14 13 12 11 10 9 8 7 6 5 4 3 2 1

89 90 91 92 93 /

CONTENTS

ILLUSTRATIONS

CHANGING VIEWS OF OURSELVES
IN THE UNIVERSE

We shall not cease from exploration
And the end of all our exploring
Will be to arrive where we started
And know the place for the first time...

T. S. Eliot

Chapter 1

CAPTAIN STORMFIELD'S VISIT TO HEAVEN

**MARK
TWAIN**

One night I was sailing along, when I discovered a tremendous long row of blinking lights away on the horizon ahead. As I approached, they begun to tower and swell and look like mighty furnaces. Says I to myself—

"By George, I've arrived at last—and at the wrong place, just as I expected!"

Then I fainted. I don't know how long I was insensible, but it must have been a good while, for, when I came to, the darkness was all gone and there was the loveliest sunshine and the balmiest, fragrantest air in its place. And there was such a marvelous world spread out before me—such a glowing, beautiful, bewitching country. The things I took for furnaces were gates, miles high, made all of flashing jewels, and they pierced a wall of solid gold that you couldn't see the top of, nor yet the end of, in either direction. I was pointed straight for one of these gates, and a-coming like a house afire. Now I noticed that the skies were black with millions of people, pointed for those gates. What a roar they made, rushing through the air! The ground was as thick as ants with people, too—billions of them, I judge.

I lit. I drifted up to a gate with a swarm of people, and when it was my turn the head clerk says, in a businesslike way—

"Well, quick! Where are you from?"

"San Francisco," says I.

"San Fran—*what?*" says he.

"San Francisco."

He scratched his head and looked puzzled, then he says—

"Is it a planet?"

By George, Peters, think of it! *"Planet?"* says I; "it's a city. And moreover, it's one of the biggest and finest and—"

"There, there!" says he, "no time for conversation. We don't deal in cities here. Where are you from in a *general* way?"

"Oh," I says, "I beg your pardon. Put me down for California."

I had him *again,* Peters! He puzzled a second, then he says, sharp and irritable—

"I don't know any such planet—is it a constellation?"

"Oh, my goodness!" says I. "Constellation, says you? No—it's a State."

"Man, we don't deal in States here. *Will* you tell me where you are from *in general—at large,* don't you understand?"

"Oh, now I get your idea," I says. "I'm from America,—the United States of America."

Peters, do you know I had him *again?* If I hadn't I'm a clam! His face was as blank as a target after a militia shooting-match. He turned to an under clerk and says—

"Where is America? *What* is America?"

The under clerk answered up prompt and says—

"There ain't any such orb."

"*Orb?*" says I. "Why, what are you talking about, young man? It ain't an orb; it's a country; it's a continent. Columbus discovered it; I reckon likely you've heard of *him,* anyway. America—why, sir, America—"

"Silence!" says the head clerk. "Once for all, where—are—you—*from?*"

"Well," says I, "I don't know anything more to say—unless I lump things, and just say I'm from the world."

"Ah," says he, brightening up, "now that's something like! *What* world?"

Peters, he had *me,* that time. I looked at him, puzzled, he looked at me, worried. Then he burst out—

"Come, come, what world?"

Says I, "Why, *the* world, of course."

"*The* world!" he says. "H'm! there's billions of them! . . . Next!"

That meant for me to stand aside. I done so, and a sky-blue man with seven heads and only one leg hopped into my place. I took a walk. It just occurred to me, then, that all the myriads I had seen swarming to that gate, up to this time, were just like that creature. I tried to run across somebody I was acquainted with, but they were out of acquaintances of mine just then. So I thought the thing all over and finally sidled back there pretty meek and feeling rather stumped, as you may say.

"Well?" said the head clerk.

"Well, sir," I says, pretty humble, "I don't seem to make out which world it is I'm from. But you may know it from this—it's the one the Saviour saved."

He bent his head at the Name. Then he says, gently—

"The worlds He has saved are like to the gates of heaven in number—none can count them. What astronomical system is your world in?—perhaps that may assist."

"It's the one that has the sun in it—and the moon—and Mars"—he shook his head at each name—hadn't ever heard of them, you see—"and Neptune —and Uranus—and Jupiter—"

"Hold on!" says he—"hold on a minute! Jupiter . . . Jupiter . . . Seems to me we had a man from there eight or nine hundred years ago—but people from that system very seldom enter by this gate." All of a sudden he begun to look me so straight in the eye that I thought he was going to bore through me. Then he says, very deliberate, "Did you come *straight here* from your system?"

"Yes, sir," I says—but I blushed the least little bit in the world when I said it.

He looked at me very stern, and says—

"This is not true; and this is not the place for prevarication. You wandered from your course. How did that happen?"

Says I, blushing again—

"I'm sorry, and I take back what I said, and confess. I raced a little with a comet one day—only just the least little bit—only the tiniest lit—"

"So—so," says he—and without any sugar in his voice to speak of.

I went on, and says—

"But I only fell off just a bare point, and I went right back on my course again the minute the race was over."

"No matter—that divergence has made all this trouble. It has brought you to a gate that is billions of leagues from the right one. If you had gone to your own gate they would have known all about your world at once and there would have been no delay. But we will try to accommodate you." He turned to an under clerk and says—

"What system is Jupiter in?"

"I don't remember, sir, but I think there is such a planet in one of the little new systems away out in one of the thinly worlded corners of the universe. I will see."

He got a balloon and sailed up and up and up, in front of a map that was as big as Rhode Island. He went on up till he was out of sight, and by and by he came down and got something to eat and went up again. To cut a long story short, he kept on doing this for a day or two, and finally he came down and said he thought he had found that solar system, but it might be fly-specks. So he got a microscope and went back. It turned out better than he feared. He had rousted out our system, sure enough. He got me to describe our planet and its distance from the sun, and then he says to his chief—

"Oh, I know the one he means, now, sir. It is on the map. It is called the Wart."

"Says I to myself, "Young man, it wouldn't be wholesome for you to go down *there* and call it the Wart."

Well, they let me in, then, and told me I was safe forever and wouldn't have any more trouble.

Chapter 2

OUR PLACE IN SPACE

Mark Twain was famous for his exaggerations, but how much exaggerating did he really allow himself when his Captain Stormfield explored the universe? Consider some of the facts that science offers us: Light travels at the rate of 186,000 miles per second—a distance more than seven times around the world. A light-year is about 6 billion, billion miles. The nearest star is more than four light-years away. By comparison, distances within our solar system are short. Light from the moon reaches Earth in less than one and a half seconds, and light from the sun crosses the intervening 93 million miles to Earth in just over eight minutes.

Philosopher Huston Smith provides additional ways for us to think about the magnitude of the universe we inhabit:

> Take the time-span that separates us from Christ and multiply it, not 50 times, but 50,000 times, and you have the approximate time it takes for a beam of light to move from one end of our galaxy to the other. . . . Andromeda, our second closest neighboring galaxy, is one-and-a-half million light years removed, beyond which the universe falls away abysmally, range after range, world after world, island universe after island universe. . . . It's enough to make one dizzy; enough to make the mind reel, and spin, and cry out for a stop. From the vantage point of our ordinary senses the vision is incredible—utterly, absolutely, completely, incredible. Only, of course, it is true.

Throughout human history we have not been much concerned with our place in space. Enough problems of survival have kept our attention on our own planet. So while the universe went its own way, people on Earth created their own ways of living—different ways in different places.

For most of our history, we have believed that the Earth is the center of the universe. This geocentric theory (*geo-*, Greek for earth; *centric* for center) was formulated as early as the fourth century B.C. by Aristotle and later "proved" (or approved) by the second-century astronomer Ptolemy. But it was also considered to be a common-sense view by anyone who looked at the sun "rising" and "setting." People feel more important when they believe themselves to be in the center of things. So it was easy, visually and psychologically, for people to assume that the Earth was the center of the universe.

In the 1500s another astronomer, Copernicus, challenged this theory, claiming that the sun, not the Earth, was the center. His findings were denounced, not because his statistics seemed in error but because his theory was an unwelcome one. People preferred to believe that the Earth was in the center. At that time, all authorities—religious, political, and educational—agreed that the geocentric view was the correct one.

The physical reality of nature, however, was on Copernicus's side. Eventually his superior predictions about movements in the heavens forced a revision of accepted ideas. Modern astronomers continued to revise the heliocentric theory (*helios* is the Greek word for sun) described by Copernicus. Using equipment such as radio telescopes and computers, sky watchers now report that our sun is a tiny, ordinary star among the billions in one galaxy, the Milky Way. And the sun is probably tens of thousands of light-years from the center of that one galaxy, which itself is probably one among hundreds or even thousands of millions of galaxies. Reluctantly, we have had to consider viewing our place in space as not being in the center of things—not being where we would prefer it to be. Even though we accept this scientific proof, we still talk about sunsets and sunrises—not about earthsets and earthrises. Our language continues to carry many reminders of the geocentric viewpoint.

Eventually, however, scientists tend to accept new findings that are based on observation and measurement. New facts usually lead to new theories; new theories usually lead to new facts.

MIND-SETS ARE NOT EASILY CHANGED

In the world of the social sciences there is an opposite tendency, called **culture lag:** new observations and new facts often reinforce old theories. Most often, our eyes and our other senses serve as filters. What we finally perceive is what our cultural screens allow to enter our minds. We need to avoid what Professor Neil Postman calls "thinking by definition." He tells this story as an example of how we tend to perceive evidence according to our definitions:

A man was sent to a psychiatrist because he believed he was dead. "Do dead men bleed?" asked the psychiatrist. "Of course not," replied the man. The psychiatrist then jabbed him in the arm with a sharp needle. For a moment, as he watched the blood ooze from his arm, the man seemed puzzled, even disappointed. Then his face brightened, he regained his composure and said, "Well, imagine that. Dead men do bleed!"

When the five-hundredth anniversary of Copernicus's birth was celebrated in 1973, the tributes went beyond recognition of his contributions to astronomy. His courage and persistence prepared the way for other scientists to report and examine findings based on facts rather than on wishes. Galileo later said that he greatly admired those who had accepted the Copernican system in spite of their common sense. For when Copernicus revealed his heliocentric theory in 1543, people were being asked to believe something that was contrary to their experience.

Now, humankind is again being forced to change its views of itself. Never before have we had the opportunity to know so much about the world and the universe we inhabit—our peoples, our natural resources, our potential technological development. Earthmen landing on the moon have perceived what poets, philosophers, and prophets have proclaimed through the centuries—the oneness of the human family. One astronaut reported:

> The view of the earth from the moon fascinated me—a small disk, 240,000 miles away. It was hard to think that that little thing held so many problems, so many frustrations. Raging nationalistic interests, famines, wars, pestilence don't show from that distance. I'm convinced that some wayward stranger in a spacecraft, coming from another part of the heavens, could look at earth and never know that it was inhabited at all. But the same wayward stranger would certainly know instinctively that if the earth were inhabited, then the destinies of all who lived on it must be inevitably interwoven and joined. We are one hunk of ground, water, air, clouds, floating around in space. From out there it really is one world.

By learning how human beings have developed and why we behave as we do, we can learn more about the processes by which human societies form their attitudes and actions. The survival and fulfillment of earthly life depend on the degree to which we can become masters rather than victims, of our own behavior. As T. S. Eliot says:

> Time present and time past
> Are both perhaps present in time future
> And time future contained in time past.

What do we need to know about "time present and time past"? Let us begin with where we have been. How has humankind until now perceived itself on earth? While we have been geocentric about our place in space, we have been *ethnocentric* (*ethnos-,* Greek for nation) about our place on Earth.

Chapter 3

OUR PLACE ON EARTH

**MARSHALL
G. S. HODGSON**

In the sixteenth century the Italian missionary, Matteo Ricci, brought to China a European map of the world showing the new discoveries in America. The Chinese were glad to learn about America, but one aspect of the map offended them. Since the map split the earth's surface down the Pacific, China appeared off at the righthand edge; whereas the Chinese thought of themselves as literally the "Middle Kingdom," which should be in the center of the map. Ricci pacified them by drawing another map, splitting the Atlantic instead, so that China appeared more central, and maps are still commonly drawn that way in that part of the world.

Europeans, of course, have clung to the first type of map, showing Europe in the upper center; while the commonest maps in North America show the United States in that post of honor, even at the cost of splitting a continent in two.

THE ANCIENT CHINESE VIEW OF THE WORLD

Many Chinese used to suppose that the Temple of Heaven at the Emperor's capital, Peking, marked the exact center of the earth's surface. To be sure, Chinese scholars even in the Middle Ages were aware that China could not be said to be mathematically central; they knew the general lay of Europe and Africa and the Indian Ocean, and a writer could remark that the "center" of the earth was along the equator. Nevertheless, even for sober historians, the pivotal fact of human history was the condition of the great Chinese empire, in which was concentrated all the splendor of polished civilization.

It could in fact be claimed that for a time China was the wealthiest and most populous, the most aesthetically cultivated and even the most powerful state on the earth.

THE WORLD VIEW FROM
MEDIEVAL INDIA

For the medieval (700–1500) Hindu the world was a place for the purification of souls. Kings and their empires came and went, the gods themselves arose and perished—time was infinite, space immense, with unlimited opportunity for every soul to reap in birth after rebirth what it had sown. In much of the universe, indeed, souls dwelt in untroubled bliss; it was the distinction of our own toiling, earthly regions that here men could choose responsibly between good and evil and their consequences. Here life was arranged for the exercise of virtue, each caste of men having its own function in society; if a man fulfilled one role well, in another life he would have a higher role to play, and might eventually rise beyond existence altogether.

The Hindu could know that there in the central lands where the sacred Ganges flowed he could live the way of truth and holiness—inaccessible to lesser breeds of men—and aspire to the highest degrees of rebirth.

THE WORLD VIEW FROM
THE MIDDLE EAST

To the medieval Muslim the world looked very different from what it did to his Chinese or to his Hindu contemporaries. History was not a matter of the varying strength and weakness of an imperial center of authority and civilization, nor was it a passing incident in an infinite succession of worlds. Rather, it was the story of a single species created just some 5,000 years ago by God to do His will once for all. From Adam on, God had sent thousands of prophets to the various peoples, bringing to each its laws and sciences; at last he sent Mohammed, proclaiming the final law in which all earlier truth was perfected and which was gradually to prevail over the whole world, replacing all former laws.

Many Muslims believed that Mohammed's birthplace, Mecca, was the center of the earth's surface. To Mecca, men pilgrimaged yearly from the farthest parts of the earth, and it was supposed that in the heavens above it the angels themselves performed worship; here was the very throne of God, where heaven and earth were nearest. To be sure, scholars knew that the earth was a sphere, and God equally present everywhere in the hearts of the believers. But their more sober picture of the world was equally effective in supporting the eminence of Islam. They thought of the inhabited quarter of the globe as a land mass lying between the equator and the North Pole, and between the oceans to the west and to the east—roughly Eurasia and northern Africa.

THE MEDIEVAL WEST EUROPEAN VIEW

The West Europeans of the same age had many of the same ideas of history and geography as the Muslims, getting them from the same Greek and Hebrew sources; but their interpretation was very different. For them history was the story of God's progressive dispensations of law or of grace to his favored people. Out of the descendants of Adam, God first chose the Hebrews, but with the coming of Christ it was the Christians who received His favors.

The West Europeans allowed that the center of the world's surface was Jerusalem (by exaggerating the length of the Mediterranean, their maps could show Spain and China as equally distant from it); but they assured themselves that, just as at the beginning of history Paradise was in the east where the sun rises, so in these latter days the center of God's vicarship on earth was in the west, where the sun sets; henceforth Rome was the center of all authority, spiritual and temporal.

THE MODERN VIEW

In modern times all these medieval pictures of the world have vanished, or been modified. With the discovery of America and the circumnavigation of the globe, the discovery that Earth is a tiny planet in an immensity of space, that mankind has been upon it hundreds of thousands of years and is still a newcomer, we have had to rethink our situation.

The West Europeans were the first to be really faced with the new discoveries and have consequently led the way toward creating a new picture of the world. But they have not yet escaped the temptation to make geography and history center upon themselves.

The map ordinarily selected to show the world as a whole is ideally suited to reinforce this way of seeing mankind. On the Mercator world map not only is Europe in the upper center; it is represented as a good deal larger than the other great culture areas. Most of these lie south of the fortieth parallel, while Europe is almost wholly north of it, where Mercator's projection begins to exaggerate the size of things enormously.

Accordingly even on the world map, which ought to provide a sense of proportion, there is space to name a great many places in Europe, while in other populous centers like India or China, shown on a much smaller scale, only a few chief places need be indicated. Although equal-area projections of the world have long been available, in which shapes as well as sizes are much less distorted, Westerners understandably cling to a projection which so markedly flatters them. They explain (as if they were engaged in nothing but sailing) that the true angles given on the Mercator map are of convenience to navigators; and in atlases and wall-maps, in books of reference and in newspapers, when Westerners turn to see what the world looks like as a whole, their preconceptions are authoritatively gratified.

In Western thinking—and this thinking still dominates too greatly other parts of the world as well—the West was the center of the world; and the world at large was to be regarded, historically most especially, in the light of its effect upon and contributions to the modern West.

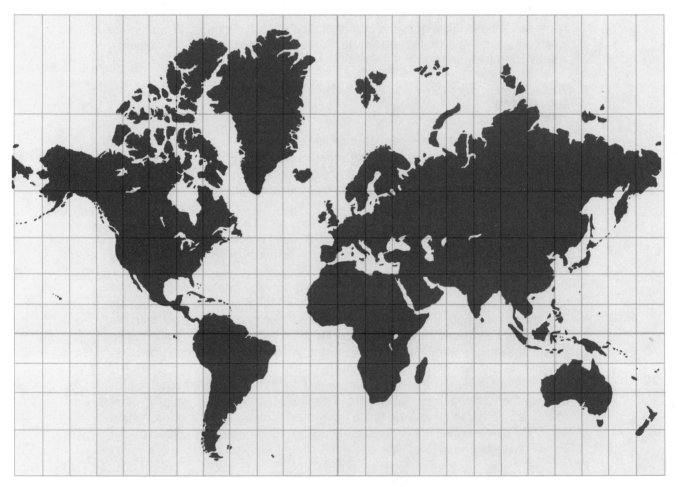

MERCATOR PROJECTION

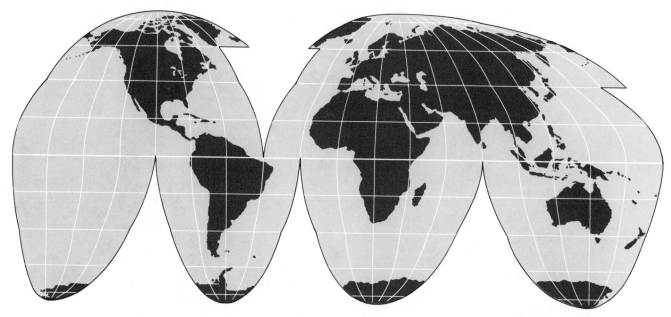

GOODE'S EQUAL-AREA PROJECTION

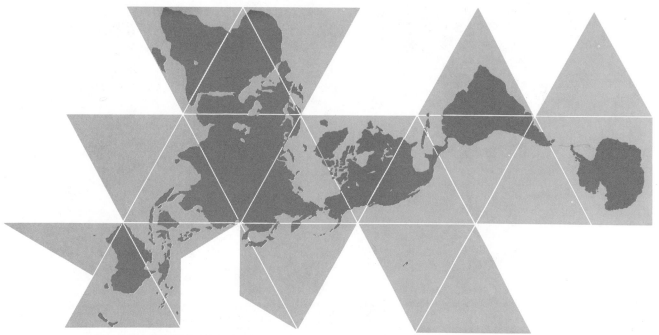

FULLER'S DYMAXION AIR-OCEAN MAP

All good people agree,
And all good people say,
All nice people like Us are We
And everyone else is They:

But if you cross over the sea,
Instead of over the way,
You may end by [think of it!]
      looking on We
As only a sort of They!

Rudyard Kipling

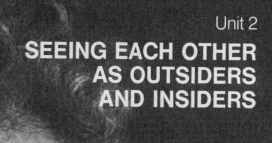

Chapter 4

INTERPRETING A FOREIGN CULTURE:

THE NACIREMA

**HORACE
MINER**

The anthroplogist has become so familiar with the diversity of ways in which different peoples behave in similar situations that he is not apt to be surprised by even the most exotic customs. In fact, if all of the logically possible combinations of behavior have not been found somewhere in the world, he is apt to suspect that they must be present in some yet undescribed tribe. . . . In this light, the magical beliefs and practices of the Nacirema present such unusual aspects that it seems desirable to describe them as an example of the extremes to which human behavior can go.

They are a North American group living in the territory between the Canadian Cree, the Yaqui and Tarahumara of Mexico, and the Carib and Arawak of the Antilles. Little is known of their origin, although tradition states that they came from the east. According to Nacirema mythology, their nation was originated by a culture hero, Notgnihsaw, who is otherwise known for two great feats of strength—the throwing of a piece of wampum across the river Pa-To-Mac and the chopping down of a cherry tree in which the Spirit of Truth resided.

Nacirema culture is characterized by a highly developed market economy which has evolved in a rich natural habitat. While much of the people's time is devoted to economic pursuits, a large part of the fruits of these labors and a considerable portion of the day are spent in ritual activity. The focus of this activity is the human body, the appearance and health of which loom as a dominant concern of the people. While such a concern is certainly not unusual, its ceremonial aspects and associated philosophy are unique.

The fundamental belief underlying the whole system appears to be that the human body is ugly and that its natural tendency is to debility and disease. Incarcerated in such a body, man's only hope is to avert these characteristics through the use of powerful influences of ritual and ceremony. Every household has one or more shrines devoted to this purpose.

The focal point of the shrine is a box or chest which is built into the wall. In this chest are kept the many charms and magical potions without which no native believes he could live. These preparations are secured from a variety of specialized practitioners. The most powerful of these are the medicine men, whose assistance must be rewarded with substantial gifts. However, the medicine men do not provide the curative potions for their clients, but decide what the ingredients should be and then write them down in ancient and secret language. This writing is understood only by the medicine men and by the herbalists who, for another gift, provide the required charm.

The charm is not disposed of after it has served its purpose, but is placed in the charm-box of the household shrine. As these magical materials are specific for certain ills, and the real or imagined maladies of the people are many, the charm-box is usually full to overflowing. The magical packets are so numerous that people forget what their purposes were and fear to use them again. While the natives are very vague on this point, we can only assume that the idea in retaining all the old magical materials is that their presence in the

box, before which the body rituals are conducted, will in some way protect the worshipper.

The Nacirema culture has an important kind of practitioner, known as a "listener." This witch doctor has the power to exorcise the devils that lodge in the heads of people who have been bewitched. The Nacirema believe that parents bewitch their own children. Mothers are particularly suspected of putting a curse on children while teaching them the secret body ritual. The counter-magic of the witch doctor is unusual in its lack of ritual. The patient simply tells the listener all his troubles and fears, beginning with the earliest difficulties he can remember. The memory displayed by the Nacirema in these exorcism sessions is truly remarkable. It is not uncommon for the patient to bemoan the rejection he felt upon being weaned as a babe, and a few individuals even see their troubles going back to the traumatic effects of their own birth.

The ritual life of the Nacirema has certainly shown them to be a magic-ridden people. It is hard to understand how they have managed to exist so long under the burdens which they have imposed upon themselves.

Chapter 5

OBSERVATIONS THROUGH THE CULTURAL LOOKING GLASS

Within the next hour about 15,000 babies will be born. At the moment of birth, the infants will be more like each other than they ever will be again. Their differences will grow because each of them is born into a different family and into a different culture—into a way of living that has developed in a particular place over a long period of time. From birth onward, each child is encouraged to be **ethnocentric**—to believe that his homeland, his people, his language, his everything is not only different but also superior to that of other people. The elders teach that the ways in which *we* do things are the natural ways, the proper ways, and the moral ways. In other places, they—"barbarians" and "foreigners"—follow a strange way of life. Ours is *the* culture; theirs is *a* culture.

This kind of behavior in favor of one's own culture occurs most frequently when groups of people live in relative isolation from each other. Survival of the group is believed to depend mainly on each person's acceptance of and loyalty to the group's traditional patterns of life and thought. People from outside the group are unwelcome because their manners and morals, being different, might by example threaten the existing system. These outsiders, in almost all languages, are designated by a word which means "stranger"—one whose beliefs and behavior are, to the insider, strange, peculiar, eccentric, erratic, odd, queer, quaint, or outlandish. This hatred of foreigners has a name; it is **xenophobia**. The anthropologists even have a name for this kind of behavior; it is **miseonism**, a deep and unreasoned hatred of new ideas. The traditional distrust of foreigners has been intensified by the news media where usually, as Marshall McLuhan observes, "real news is bad news—bad news *about* somebody or bad news *for* somebody." We have been generally conditioned to think of other national groups as either threats or burdens. Terms such as "trouble spots," "powder kegs," and "points of conflict" are often used to describe situations and conditions outside the United States. Such terms carry the feeling that the rest of the world has become a "burdensome" and "trouble-some" place which creates a continuous series of problems for us.

Deaths and population decreases among foreigners are often unconsciously welcomed as "good news" because of the feeling that there will be fewer of "them" with whom to compete for worldly resources, which are assumed to be limited. Because each nation tends to exaggerate its own achievements, people everywhere tend not to appreciate how much of their own development—in ideas and in physical survival—has been contributed by "foreigners."

In some ways, however, the ethnocentric view of life is "right"; the pattern of responses that evolved in a particular place may make relatively good sense —for *that* particular people and place. This generalization was especially true in the past when, according to Professor Elting E. Morison:

> For generations—for centuries—men did their work with the natural resources and energies lying ready at hand—the earth, the beast of burden, the wind and falling water. These materials and sources of power remained on the whole con-stant and stable; therefore the conditioned reflexes, habits of mind, customary emotional responses—in short, the culture—built up around these agencies re-mained on the whole relatively constant and stable.

SEPARATE AND RELATED

As human beings become aware of their relatedness, they need not necessarily cease being ethnocentric. When a person begins to identify with a nation, he does not cease being a member of his immediate family; he learns to apportion and extend his loyalties. Ethnocentrism is important and useful because it helps a person to develop a local cultural pattern that is appropriate for specific conditions. It would be unfortunate if the richness of cultural variety were lost to us. In learning about other cultures, the objective is not to discover a "universal culture" suitable for all people, in all places, and for all times. Rather, the ob-jective is to learn the lesson that Aldous Huxley described following his first around-the-world trip in 1926:

> So the journey is over and I am back again, richer by much experience and poorer by many exploded convictions, many perished certainties. For convictions and certainties are too often the concomitants of ignorance. . . . I set out on my travels knowing, or thinking I knew, how men should live, how be governed, how educated, what they should believe. I had my views on every activity of life. Now, on my return, I find myself without any of these pleasing certainties. . . . The better you understand the significance of any question, the more difficult it becomes to answer it. Those who attach a high importance to their own opinion should stay at home. When one is traveling, convictions are mislaid as easily as spectacles, but unlike spectacles, they are not easily replaced.

A person's awareness of his own ethnocentricity does not mean that he therefore must consider all cultures equally acceptable to him. Awareness can, however, help an observer to realize that what he "sees" is largely already "behind his eyes." Marshall McLuhan says, "Our need today is, culturally, the same as the scientist's who seeks to become aware of the bias of the instruments of research in order to correct that bias." A similar warning comes from Pierre Teilhard de Chardin: "When researchers reach the end of their analysis, they cannot tell with any certainty whether the structure they have made is the essence of the matter they are studying, or the reflection of their own thoughts."

Today, humankind is living in a world where groups are becoming more and more interrelated, less and less isolated. Ignorance of others is *not* bliss and what you don't know *can* hurt you. Moreover, many inventions and styles of life created by individual groups can help others. Each culture does not have to reinvent the wheel or depend exclusively on its own scientists, philosophers, and artists. Learning about other cultures is not something done as a favor to the people who live in them—as an expression of goodwill. Such knowledge can be of immediate and profound benefit and pleasure to the learner.

We should, in the words of James Thurber, "not look back in anger or look forward in fear but look around in awareness." It is too late for us to be unprejudiced, but we can recognize and become alert to our condition. The unprejudiced mind is not without prejudices; it is, says Hans Selye, "a mentality that has control over its numerous prejudices, and is always willing to reconsider them in the face of contrary evidence."

For example, in the United States the currently popular way of dividing the world is in terms of Western and non-Western cultures. In the so called non-Western parts of the globe are people as different from each other as Chinese, Indians, Nigerians, Egyptians, and Iranians. But these differences are minimized or, more often, overlooked or ignored. In a similar way, all the peoples who were living in the Americas when Columbus landed were identified by the Europeans as "Indians." The so-called Indians never thought of themselves as one people but considered themselves, more correctly, to be Iroquois, Hopi, Aztecs, Incas, and other tribal groups.

The major purposes, therefore, of learning about other cultures is to discover the ways in which other groups of human beings have organized their lives to answer the perennial questions of survival and fulfillment. Confucius said, "The nature of people is always the same; it is their habits which separate them."

FACTS AND FEELINGS

Each culture has its own kinds of achievements and problems. In comparing his country to the United States, an educated person from India, for example, would not deny that his country is backward with reference to the number of the reasons are no longer relevant, changes can be introduced without serious damage to the cultural pattern. Many times, however, the relevance of traditional customs is not understood by outsiders. Changes introduced under these conditions are often harmful.

As another example of a point of view based on cultural context, consider that in the United States the automobile holds a special (some would say "sacred") position, even though over 2 million Americans have died in motor vehicle crashes since their invention—almost twice the number killed in all of our wars. Each year, about 46,000 people in this country die in car accidents—a rate of one every eleven minutes. The number seriously injured annually is over 2 million. The total economic loss is estimated at $50 billion yearly.

If a "non-Western" consultant were to study "the problem of the automobile in the United States" he might start out by considering it basically as a means of transportation. After all, this is how Henry Ford started out when he produced all of his earliest cars in one color and changed models only when there were technological advances. In terms of transportation, the consultant might recommend that we have fewer cars and more express trains and that in fact we should consider "birth control" of cars because they are increasing so rapidly in number. In making this recommendation, however, the foreign consultant would reveal a lack of understanding of the car's place in American culture. The American economy currently depends overwhelmingly on widespread auto transportation, and the car is believed to be an essential part of an American's "pursuit of happiness."

One of the best ways to see one's own culture is through the eyes of an outsider. In the following "might-have-been" research article, a college student reports on another important activity in the life of the Nacirema:

Chapter 6

THE SACRED "RAC"

PATRICIA HUGHES

An Indian anthropologist, Chandra Thapar, made a study of foreign cultures which had customs similar to those of his native land. One culture in particular fascinated him because it reveres one animal as sacred, much as the people in India revere the cow. The things he discovered might interest you since you will be studying India as part of this course.

The tribe Dr. Thapar studied is called the Asu and is found on the American continent north of the Tarahumara of Mexico. Though it seems to be a highly developed society of its type, it has an overwhelming preoccupation with the care and feeding of the rac—an animal much like a bull in size, strength and temperament. In the Asu tribe, it is almost a social obligation to own at least one if not more racs. Anyone not possessing at least one is held in low esteem by the community because he is too poor to maintain one of these beasts properly. Some members of the tribe, to display their wealth and social prestige, even own herds of racs.

Unfortunately the rac breed is not very healthy and usually does not live more than five to seven years. Each family invests large sums of money each year to keep its rac healthy and shod, for it has a tendency to throw its shoes often. There are rac specialists in each community, perhaps more than one if the community is particularly wealthy. These specialists, however, due to the long period of ritual training they must undergo and to the difficulty of obtaining the right selection of charms to treat the rac, demand costly offerings whenever a tribesman must treat his ailing rac.

At the age of sixteen in many Asu communities, many youths undergo a puberty rite in which the rac figures prominently. The youth must petition a high priest in a grand temple. He is then initiated into the ceremonies that surround the care of the rac and is permitted to keep a rac.

Although the rac may be used as a beast of burden, it has many habits which would be considered by other cultures as detrimental to the life of the society. In the first place the rac breed is increasing at a very rapid rate and the Asu tribesmen have given no thought to curbing the rac population. As a consequence the Asu must build more and more paths for the rac to travel on since its delicate health and its love of racing other racs at high speeds necessitates that special areas be set aside for its use. The cost of smoothing the earth is too costly for any one individual to undertake; so it has become a community project and each tribesman must pay an annual tax to build new paths and maintain the old. There are so many paths needed that some people move their homes because the rac paths must be as straight as possible to keep the animal from injuring itself. Dr. Thapar also noted that unlike the cow, which many people in his country hold sacred, the excrement of the rac cannot be used as either fuel or fertilizer. On the contrary, its excrement is exceptionally foul and totally useless. Worst of all, the rac is prone to rampages in which it runs down anything in its path, much like stampeding cattle. Estimates are that the rac kills thousands of the Asu in a year.

Despite the high cost of its upkeep, the damage it does to the land, and its habit of destructive rampages, the Asu still regard it as being essential to the survival of their culture.

Chapter 7

MUCH DEPENDS ON WHAT WE ASSUME

**RAYMOND
GORDEN**

Contrary to public opinion, most cross-culture miscommunication is not due to a lack of goodwill or sensitivity on the part of the individuals involved. Instead, we have found repeatedly in our research that *meaning* is not contained in the actions or words alone. The actions or words constitute the message, which must still be *interpreted by the receiver* in the context of the particular situation. How this process works is revealed in the following fictional, but fact-based, dialogue.

This example relates the experiences of American Peace Corps trainees when cashing their checks in Bogotá, Colombia. As the trainees enter the bank, which resembles a modern American bank, they head for different tellers' windows.

Bob: We made it before they closed.

Jim: Great, but it will take a while with this crowd!

Bob: We'll have to push ahead, or we may never get to the window. It looks like the crowd waiting for a bus. There are too many people crammed in here to keep a line.

Jim: Right! But we'll make it!

Bob: (*Softly to Jim*) This guy on your right seems to be a little restless. I thought *we* were supposed to be the impatient ones.

Jim: (*Softly to Bob*) Impatient is right. He's elbowing his way ahead! Look, he stuck his check right in front of me, and I haven't even gotten my money yet!

Bob: (*Softly*) And he didn't even say pardon me! He must be a friend of the manager . . . see how the teller snapped it up?

Jim: (To the Colombian) Señor, are you in a hurry?

Colombian: No, señor, not *I,* but I thought *you* were in a hurry since you are still standing in front of the window!

Jim: Yes, but I'm still waiting for my money!

Colombian: Yes, I know, but I had to give my check to the teller.

Jim: But you don't . . .

Bob: (*Interrupting*) The teller's got your money now.

Teller: Cien pesos, dos cientos, dos cientos cincuenta, setenta, noventa, tres cientos.

Jim: Gracias, señor.

Bob: Let's bug out of here. Joe is already waiting outside.

Jim: Right! What a rude jerk! He knew damned well that I hadn't gotten my money yet!

Narrator: The trainees reassembled outside the bank and are walking back to the Training Center as they talk about their experiences inside the bank.

Bob: Wow! That guy was out of this world. He had his own way of getting ahead.

Jim: Yeah! This is the second time I've been to the bank to cash a check, and the same thing happened to me last time. I couldn't believe it at first. (*To Joe*) How did you guys do, Joe?

Joe: Well, we got our money, and that's what counts. I'm sure it was worth the trouble.

Jim: You can say that again. Last week, when I got to the head of the line at the teller's window, I gave my check to the teller and was standing there minding my own business and waiting for my money when this Colombian sort of nudged me to one side and put his check on the counter right in front of me. I was trying to decide what to do when another guy bumped me from the other side and plunked his check down in front of me. I was getting pretty sore, but I didn't say anything that time!

Joe: Today I was lucky. No one pushed in front of me.

Jim: Well, this guy today was just plain rude. He didn't want to wait for his turn!

Joe: Did he realize that you were still waiting for your money?

Jim: Yeah! I wondered about the same thing last week, so this time I got a little bolder and asked him if he was in a hurry or something. I told him that I was waiting for my money and that his turn would come next.

Joe: Did he say anything to that?

Jim: He sure did! He tried to convince me that I had already had my turn. I'm sure that is what he said. Sometimes I wonder whether these Colombians are civilized yet!

Narrator: Up to this point we have heard only the thoughts of the Americans. We know only what the Colombian said directly to the American. To obtain the Colombian point of view on this same situation, a Colombian interviewer questioned the teller who worked at the window where Jim had cashed his check that afternoon.

Interviewer: Señor Pardo, it is very kind of you to stay and talk to me after the bank has closed. As I explained to the manager, this will not take too long.

Teller: There is no problem, señor. Please sit down!

Interviewer: Gracias, señor, As you know, we are studying the problems North Americans have in getting along in Colombia. We want to develop better orientation materials for students, Peace Corps trainees, and other North Americans who visit Colombia.

Teller: Si, señora, that's a good idea!

Interviewer: How do they get along as customers in your bank?

Teller: They are rude . . . some of them!

Interviewer: In what way?

Teller: When they come in to cash their checks, some of them are rude!

Interviewer: I see. What did they *do* that was rude?

Teller: They hand their check to me and then stand right in front of the window until they get their cash!

Narrator: When the director of the research team read the transcript of the interview, he realized that the Colombian interviewer failed to reveal some important information, so he talked with the interviewer.

American: (*Rustles papers.*) Ah, here it is! In your interview with the bank teller I don't understand why he thought the customer was rude, the one who stood in front of the teller's window until he got his money.

Colombian: Well, maybe that was an exaggeration to call him rude, but he sure wasn't nice.

American: I *don't* understand what he should have done in order not to be rude.

Colombian: He just shouldn't stand there in the way.

American: In whose way?

Colombian: The other customers who want to cash their checks.

American: Just what is the customer here in Bogotá *supposed* to do when he cashes a check?

Colombian: The same as anywhere . . . in Colombia at least.

American: And what is that?

Colombian: Get out of the way so that others can have their turn.

American: But shouldn't they wait until after the first customer has had his turn?

Colombian: Of course, but that is what the teller was saying! The American had already taken his turn!

Narrator: The American realized that he was not communicating with the Colombian interviewer. The difficulty seemed to revolve around the concept of taking turns at the bank. Let us listen as he probes further into this area.

American: Did I understand correctly that the *Norteamericano* still had not received his money when the *Colombiano* put his check through the teller's window?

Colombian: That is correct.

American: Then he didn't have his turn yet, right?

Colombian: That's *not* right! He already took his turn.

American: He already took his turn?

Colombian: Yes, he already gave his check to the teller.

American: But he hasn't gotten his money!

Colombian: No, because the teller has not called his name yet!

American: Why should the teller call his name? He just handed him the check with his name on it, and he's still standing right in front of the teller!

Colombian: But, the teller has to wait for the check to be approved before he can cash it, and in the meantime the *Norteamericano* should let the other customers have their turn to give their checks to the teller so that he can send them along for approval.

American: Oh! Then is this the way it works? The customer goes to the window, hands the check to the teller, steps back from the window so that others can step up and give their checks to the teller, and then when his check is approved for cashing, the teller will call his name.

Colombian: Exactly!

American: Then why form a line?

Colombian: We don't . . . and shouldn't because it would make the system much less efficient!

Narrator: We have heard that "We don't form a line . . . that would be inefficient." *That* statement completes the information gathered from the people directly involved in the situation. Let's pause to analyze what we have learned from the whole case.

We have learned that in Bogotá it is assumed that the customer will walk to the teller directly, hand him the check, step away from the window, wait to hear his named called, then return to the teller's cage to get his money. Very simple when we know the rules of the game. In the context of these rules, the Colombians' conversation made sense. The Colombian interviewer said that if each customer stood in line and stayed at the window until he received his cash, the check-cashing procedure would be very inefficient.

As North Americans, we have learned to associate lining up for services with orderliness, discipline, efficiency, and democracy. It is hard for us to believe that a bank could give more efficient service to customers who do *not* line up to take turns in receiving their money. Yet this is true. The concept of the line was so firmly implanted in the minds of the North Americans that they could report in all honesty that they had stood in line when actually there was no line to stand in. What looks to the Colombians like a group of people around the teller's window looks to the North Americans like a line pushing its way through a group.

The important point here is that many of the differences between two cultures in a given face-to-face interaction are due to differences in the larger institutional structure of which the interaction is a part. The interaction between customer and teller in cashing a check in a particular bank is a part of the larger nationwide banking system. The bank customer in any culture rarely knows the whole system, but he must learn at least those patterns of behavior relevant to his particular role in the system. The banking system in Latin America is totally different in its structure from the system in the United States. Not only must the customer act differently, but so must the teller, the bookkeeper, the manager, the board of directors, the guard, the stockholders, and the government officials—all must act differently to make the system function.

Unconsciously, the North American assumes that the banking procedures work so that the customers receive their cash in the same order they give their checks to the teller. This is true in the United States because the teller himself usually makes the decision to cash a particular check or not. The Colombian teller can never make this decision alone. Instead, he verifies that the check is properly made out, that it has been endorsed, and then he passes it along to others who determine whether there are funds to cover the check. They deduct the amount of the check from the account and then record the new balance on the monthly statement sheet. This whole bookkeeping operation is completed efficiently with modern office machines *before* the customer receives his cash. This system makes it impossible for an account to be overdrawn. Latin American bank tellers find it incredible that North American bankers would actually let their tellers hand out cash first and then do the bookkeeping later only to discover that some accounts are overdrawn.

Yet, in the U.S. system, there is no foolproof way to avoid overdrawing an account at a particular bank, because checks charged against that account may be cashed at *other* banks, then routed through a clearinghouse to the bank holding the account. An account cannot be overdrawn in Latin America because a check must be cashed at the bank holding the account against which the check was issued. There is no clearinghouse arrangement between banks. This makes it inconvenient for a person who has received payment in checks drawn upon several different banks, because he must go to each of the banks in turn to cash the corresponding checks.

You will never advance far in your
understanding of another culture if you
devote yourself to exclaiming that
some things about it are wonderful and other
things are terrible. This comes under
the heading of entertainment and should not
be confused with understanding. No society is
all good or all bad, and the discovery that
any particular society is compounded of both
good and bad is not a very impressive finding.
What you must try to do is to understand
what problems a society faces; why it has
developed the way it has; why it has certain
characteristics rather than others; why it does
some things so well and other things
very badly.

John W. Gardner

Chapter 8

SIX SUGGESTIONS FOR LEARNING ABOUT PEOPLES AND CULTURES

YU-KUANG
CHU

Although the illustrative examples in this article are drawn from Asia, an area of the world the writer knows best, the basic principles can be applied to other regions as well. At least six necessary attitudes or abilities should be considered:

ONE **Beware of stereotyped views of foreign peoples.** The word *stereotype* is defined in the dictionary as "a process for making a plate of typed metal" which can be used for reproducing identical copies. People are also often "stereotyped" into categories: "all Negroes are musical, lazy, superstitious"; "all lawyers are crooked"; "all Chinese are mysterious." Stereotypes are shortcuts in thinking and abbreviated guides to action. As such they are natural to the human mind, and some amount of stereotyping is perhaps unavoidable. However, many popular notions are entirely false and others, though having an element of truth, are sweeping oversimplifications. The chief trouble with even valid stereotypes is that they may not apply to a particular individual.

> Whether favorable or unfavorable, a stereotype is an exaggerated belief associated with a category. Its function is to justify (rationalize) our conduct in relation to that belief. . . . The stereotype acts both as a device for justifying acceptance or rejection of a group, and as a screening device to maintain simplicity in perception and in thinking.
>
> A stereotype is sustained by selective perception and selective forgetting. When a Jew achieves a goal, we may say quite automatically, "The Jews are so clever." If he fails to achieve the goal, we say nothing—not thinking to amend our stereotype. In the same way we may overlook nine neat Negro householders, but triumphantly exclaim when we encounter the slovenly tenth, "they do ruin property."

Gordon W. Allport

TWO   **See the common humanity of people amidst cultural diversities in the world.**   Cultural studies must constantly avoid extreme emphases. One is to over-emphasize the differences between the West and the non-West to such an extent that it strengthens the popular notion that Easterners are mysterious, inscrutable, and somehow not naturally and reasonably human as we are. The other extreme is to assume that all other peoples are exactly like us so that any Western system such as democracy can be transplanted on any foreign soil provided the stubborn opposition would simply give way. We can strike a balance between these two extremes by pointing constantly to the fact that despite real and serious cultural differences people everywhere have a common humanity in their basic motivations and desires. They have different solutions to the same problems in life although they follow contrasting ways of behavior.

For example, there are many reversals of customs between here and East Asia. The family name comes before the personal name in Chinese and Japanese. A letter is addressed to the country, province, city, street, house number, and lastly the recipient. The title of a person comes after his name instead of before. There the left is the honored side, while in this country the right has the higher priority. At mixed parties in the home of the writer, Occidental friends are seated on the right and Orientals on the left. Everybody is happy. An American child sticks out his tongue to show defiance, a Tibetan to show courtesy to a stranger, a Chinese to express wonderment, and before World War II a Japanese put his tongue between his teeth and sucked in his breath, producing a hissing sound, to show extreme respect to the emperor. In all of these bewildering and amusing reversals, there is no question of superiority of one custom over another; but the establishment of a definite custom giving orderliness to life is the same.

Sometimes the equivalences are not so obvious. In most Asian stores (outside of Japan), the price of merchandise is not labeled. A customer has to pick an article and ask for the price. The merchant will ask for a sky-high price and the customer will return a rock-bottom offer. In the ensuing bargaining process the merchant's price will gradually come down and the customer's offer will slowly go up. If they meet, there will be a sale; if not, the customer walks out of the store without anybody's feelings being hurt. When the writer criticized this practice as time-wasting to an American G.I. who obviously enjoyed bargaining while he was in China during the War, the soldier said that in making a major purchase in this country one also wastes a lot of time in going from store to store in order to find the right price tag. He summed up the equivalence by saying, "We walk; you talk."

A more serious illustration has to do with insurance. In this country one spends a considerable part of one's income buying all sorts of insurance. In traditional China there were no insurance companies. Before students jump to the conclusion that there were no accidents or misfortunes in Chinese life (obviously untrue) or that the Chinese could bear any hardship without provisions for security (also untrue), they should rather assume that since Chinese are human beings and Chinese life is human life, there must be something in their culture equivalent in function to insurance. Upon careful search they will find that the extended Chinese family system did absorb the shocks of accidents or misfortunes and provide security to its members. The writer's wife is the oldest of three siblings who lost both of their parents very early in their childhood. They were automatically taken care of, without any questions asked, by a paternal uncle and his wife, who had three children of their own. The three unfortunate children were raised on exactly the same basis as the natural ones. It is not too much to say that the Chinese people were born into, worked for, and were taken care of in sickness, old age, and death by an insurance company! That the traditional family system has been breaking down under modern conditions and that insurance companies have emerged simply proves the equivalence in function in this respect between these two agencies.

THREE **Recognize a different scale of values in a non-Western society.** Although many values are universals cutting across cultural differences, yet there are differences in value systems. Students should see that in societies characterized by the absence of strong government or by the presence of precariousness or danger, social stability is much more highly prized than social change, and group solidarity is much more valued than individual freedom. A cornerstone of social stability is family solidarity. Once this value system is accepted, then many corollaries follow: respect for the aged, because in a stable society wisdom comes from accumulation of experience; marriages arranged by parents, because marriage is not the personal affair of the couple involved but a family matter profoundly affecting its welfare and integrity; the importance of male issue, to be secured, if not by the wife then by concubinage, adoption, or arrangement with a son-in-law for him to live with the wife's family and take over her family name; the punishment of the group for crimes committed by an individual of the group, because this is the simplest way to deter disruptions of the social fabric; and so forth. The contrast to dynamic Western society and values is obvious.

Here the student needs to learn to distinguish between a statement of fact and a value judgment. He must beware of the tendency to judge a non-Western culture *unconsciously* according to his own scale of values.

FOUR **Develop human empathy and active concern for other peoples.** Education is a process continuously extending human sympathy and understanding in time and space—for one's immediate family through the community and nation to the world and from the present backwards to the remote past and forwards into the future. Students should be led to see human problems on a world scale and feel ethical obligations on the international level. They need to see how various civilizations had their golden ages at different times in different parts of the world and contributed to the sum of human civilization. While Western civilization seems to ride on the crest of the wave now, the West was once culturally indebted to peoples beyond the West—to Arabs for their scholarship as well as their preservation of classical Greek learning during the Dark Ages, to the Jews for the Judaic-Christian tradition and ethic, to the Chinese for three inventions, among other things, which facilitated the transformation of feudal Europe into modern Europe—gunpowder, paper, and the compass. For the West now to help the economically poor nations is in part a repayment of a cultural debt in much the same way as a man repays his debt to his parents by raising his own children.

FIVE **Discern the inter-relationships between language and culture.** This discernment can never be acquired if one is limited to one's own language and culture. Here non-Western studies and languages have the special advantage of affording a sharper contrast to Western counterparts, thus bringing out the problem more clearly. As is well known, language is intimately related to thinking, feeling, and acting. When one hears somebody say "Pardon me" for having made a *faux pas,* a Westerner says "Certainly," but a Chinese would say "Not at all." Both are being courteous, but the Westerner is the more frank and direct and seems to say, "Yes, you have made a slip, but since you have asked my pardon, there is no question at all about my being willing to pardon you." The Easterner, on the other hand, is the more circuitous, tries to overlook the *faux pas,* and sounds as if he is saying, "What is there to pardon? Nothing at all!"

The English way of saying "yes" or "no" is very confusing to a Chinese and vice versa unless the difference in viewpoint is made clear. In English no matter how a question is put, if the objective fact is affirmative, "yes" is the answer and if negative, "no." In Chinese, one has to watch the questioner. If the question presumes a negative answer, and the presumption is right, the proper answer is "yes," meaning "Yes, you are right." Thus, to the question, "This book is not yours, is it?" the Chinese answer may be "Yes, it is not mine." It seems, at least in this case, Westerners are more fact-oriented whereas the Chinese are more people-oriented.

SIX **Finally, study cultures for their intrinsic worth and thus see the richness of human thought and life.** This better acquaintance with humankind will usually reduce ethnocentrism or academic provincialism. An art student seeing how Chinese painters use blank space as a structural element or how Japanese craftsmen create beauty out of simplicity has a fuller understanding of art. A student in philosophy exposed to the variety of Indian philosophies and religions will have a much richer view of life and reality. A student of literature will delight in discovering "new" (to Westerners) forms and techniques of literary expression in Asian writings.

Chapter 9

HOW ATTITUDES ARE SOMETIMES FORMED

PHILIP FOSTER

Our ignorance of Africa is partly due to the fact that it was one of the last areas to be opened up by Western penetration and exploration. To be sure, Arab explorers knew some of the lands south of the Sahara, but vast sections of the continent's interior lay unseen by European eyes due to poor coastal harbors, the difficulty of traveling to the interior, and in some areas, the presence of widespread tropical disease.

The hazards of early African exploration are not, however, the only reason for some of our present false images of the continent and its people. Western attitudes toward Africa are formed not only from ignorance; they come also from *deliberate* self-deception. This is mainly because the first large-scale contact between Europeans and Africans was made during the period of the slave trade beginning in the sixteenth century. At that time, men's consciences were less troubled if it could be shown that African slaves were, after all, mere savages with no real culture or civilization. Indeed, it was commonly said that slavery was a good thing for Africans considering the barbaric societies from which they came. Better, it was said, to be an ill-treated slave in a "civilized" society than a free man in a primitive one. Americans, in particular, had good reason to deceive themselves about Africa, for it would have been unpleasant to admit that they were enslaving people whose civilizations were not inferior to those of their fellow men in parts of Asia, Europe, and the Americas. Unfortunately, some of these attitudes concerning Africa have persisted until today.

Recently, movies and television in particular have done little to dispel these attitudes. By showing scenes of so-called "primitive" life in Africa, too often these visualizations aim to thrill and entertain people rather than to inform them. Apart from giving an often entirely inaccurate picture of the land and its wildlife, movies and television tend to portray the African himself as an uncivilized and primitive person. The "good" African in the movies is the servant of the fearless white hunter, while the "bad" African is ferocious and treacherous. One would hardly imagine from all this nonsense that Africa has large, modern, Western-type cities, industries, universities, and schools.

Chapter 10

WHAT WE KNOW IS OFTEN NOT SO:

AFRICA AND AFRICANS

SUSAN
HALL

What picture comes to your mind when you hear the word "Africa"? Chances are it is the picture of a "Dark Continent" and all that this phrase entails. For even today our media still find an audience for their offerings of .Tarzan, Pygmies and polygamous despotic rulers. It is hard to believe that in our scientific age such myths are still perpetuated.

The "darkness" surrounding Africa is actually our ignorance of the continent. Ernest Hemingway, Robert Ruark, Joseph Conrad, H. Rider Haggard, and Edgar Rice Burroughs based their vivid, exciting novels on a romantic, exotic continent that existed primarily in their imaginations. To accept their visions and to describe Africa with words such as "dark," "cruel," "primitive," "savage," "barbaric," "backward," and "uncivilized," is to accept a bizarre fantasy world with little basis in reality. Instead of locking our minds into this perspective, let us examine some of these popular misconceptions, some blatant, some subtle, to see what truths lie behind them.

1   **Africa is mainly a land of sweltering jungles.**

Most of the continent is savanna or grassland while only about one-seventh of it is rain forest. This latter is located almost entirely in the Congo Basin, the Gulf of Guinea coast area of West Africa, and the eastern coast of the Malagasy Republic. Because of their dense foliage and the presence of cloud cover, the forests are not the hottest places on the continent; in fact, the temperature there rarely exceeds 90 degrees. The only "jungles" might be found near the river banks, where vegetation is naturally much thicker. On the other hand, the savanna region stretches from the forest zones to the desert areas, varying its growth from lush green grasses to drier coarser shrubs as the region moves away from the forest.

2 **Large numbers of wild animals—lions, leopards, elephants— can be found roaming all over, but especially in the jungles.**

Most of the game animals that are found in Africa live in the grasslands, most specifically in parks set aside and preserved, often as tourist attractions, on a small percentage of the land mainly in southern and East Africa. In fact, certain species of animals are dwindling to the point of extinction (some have already died away) because man has hunted them for sport or for their meat, skin and tusks. As a footnote, tigers are not indigenous to Africa but to Asia.

3 **Africa south of the Sahara is mainly peopled by Bushmen, Pygmies, and Watusi.**

The total population of Africa is estimated to be about 560 million people. Of this number about 435 million live south of the Sahara; included in this figure are, at most, 1.5 million Bushmen, Pygmies, Watusi and people related to them in physical characteristics and life style. Also included in this figure are at least 6 million white Africans and people of European origin who claim Africa as their home.

4 **Africans have never achieved a high level of civilization on their own, or Africa has no history until its discovery by Europeans.**

These generalizations are very much tied up with European and American racial philosophies needed as justification for slavery, and, later, for domination of one people by another both in Africa and the United States. They picture Africans with low intellectual abilities, naturally childlike personalities, and natures easily adaptable or even happy in the most stressful and unsatisfactory conditions. Scientifically, these have no basis in truth. Further, we also know that while Europeans were living in the "Dark Ages," powerful and wealthy African kingdoms were flourishing in West Africa. Beautifully crafted artifacts have been unearthed in Nigeria attesting to the ancient Nok culture there while architectural ruins chronicle the ancient trading empire of Kush in East Africa. Add to these our reverence for Egyptian civilization, the "cradle" of Western culture; scholars may still be debating the skin shades of its leaders, but it was, nevertheless, an African culture.

5 **Africans constantly engaged in fierce tribal wars before the coming of the Europeans. In fact, it was the presence of Europeans that stopped the Africans from killing one another.**

What is interesting is that almost the complete opposite it true. The arrival of European slavers increased tribal warfare while slavery and the slave trade were responsible for the loss of millions of African lives. This is not to say that wars did not exist before; they did. For most Africans, nevertheless, their traditional life was full with the business of growing food, herding cattle, worshipping God, and the daily relationships with family and friends. If disputes grew, they were sometimes settled peacefully; at other times they were solved through wars. However, with the arrival of slave traders, a few strong men allied with the Europeans and used European guns to "get rich quick" by raiding and selling their weaker neighbors, thereby increasing tribal warfare.

Often, too, accounts of the slave trade begin with the assertion that Africans practiced slavery long before Europeans began the trade. This is true, but indigenous African slavery lacked the pernicious qualities of the trade and institution controlled by the Europeans. It did not involve the slaughter, harsh treatment and wholesale transporting of people from one environment to another that the transatlantic trade entailed. Too, slaves in Africa were often able to wield political power in the societies in which they lived. In some of the famous West African kingdoms only slaves could hold certain high government positions because only they were unfettered by family obligations and considered impartial administrators. The stress on African slavery is too often a justification for our own inhumane actions.

6 **Africans lived in primitive villages with no political system, or all Africans lived in tribes headed by powerful despotic chiefs.**

All Africans had some indigenous form of political organization but there is great variety in the form this organization took. In essence, we know that some societies had chiefs, others were ruled by elaborate bureaucracies, others were led by groups of men, often elders, while still others acted in autonomous groups, independent of other segments of their people. Many chiefs and kings had a great deal of power but even they were usually subject to the group's traditional legal and religious codes. If tyranny prevailed because a ruler managed to concentrate too much power in his own hands, the leader was usually dealt with in the same manner as European despots were countered —he was defeated as he attempted to widen his empire or deposed by a popular coup. On the other hand, many societies practiced complete democracy with all adult members sharing in making major decisions and with no one person having more power than his neighbors. Probably the only generalization that can be made about traditional African political systems is that one indeed existed in every society.

7 **African men buy their wives and most men have more than one wife.**

Bridewealth or brideprice and polygamy are two of the most frequently misunderstood practices of African societies. Basic to a comprehension of their meaning is an understanding of the concept of descent groups, generally the most important unit of African society. It is in his descent group that a man finds his identity. This group or his family is composed of his parents, uncles, cousins, and other relatives. Often it is the oldest male in a descent group who settles disputes among the members. Too, it is usually the family elders who ensure that a man has enough land on which to grow food for his wife (or wives) and children. A man's relatives can also be relied upon when he needs help in his work and they will come to his aid if he is ill or when he gets too old to care for himself.

Thus, when a man marries it is not an individual affair. He is bringing into the family a woman who is part of another descent group but who will, by bearing children, enrich his group. Marriage is then a contract between two families. To show his good faith and to indicate that he will treat his wife well, a man gives bridewealth to his fiancée's family. It is token compensation to them for the loss of a daughter. Should the wife leave him, the husband gets the brideprice back. The exchange, consequently, gives both families an interest in keeping the marriage intact. (American bridewealth practices are somewhat similar. A man gives his fiancée a diamond ring to signify his love while the bride goes to her husband complete with gifts given to her by the couple's friends and their families.)

A descent group, in turn, cannot survive without children. Children ensure their parents that the family will continue, they will be cared for in their old age, and they will be honored after their death. If a man can afford it, then, he marries more than one wife so that his descent group will grow and be strengthened.

8   **Traditional Africans worshipped many gods or had no religion at all. Periodic human sacrifices were deemed necessary to keep evil spirits from harming the people.**

Europeans entered Africa in large numbers during a period when intense nationalism, national rivalries, and feelings of cultural superiority prevailed on their home continent. Few ever thought to study the dynamics of the cultures they encountered abroad. These colonial preconceptions were often reinforced by missionaries' reports in which the idea of "Christianizing the natives" was dramatized to encourage funding and support from the congregation at home. Only recently have thorough studies of African philosophical and religious systems been undertaken. From these certain similarities between belief systems seem to emerge.

Generally, man is at the center of life. Above him and over all the universe is a supreme God. Between man and God are the spirits of man's ancestors who have lived according to the tribe's laws and mores, who have learned and practiced its wisdom, and who have set an example for those on earth to follow. These ancestors act as intermediaries with God and the lesser spirits. Man venerates them, seeks their advice, and they, in turn, use their power to help their descendents. Below man in this hierarchy of beings are the plant and animal world. Though man is often more powerful than these forces, they also have life and deserve man's respect. Ideally, man lives in harmony with all the other beings, his environment and his ancestors. He does not try to conquer or control nature but rather to adapt his rhythm of life to that of the world in which he lives. For any important event—a birth, a death, an initiation into manhood, a harvest, a serious illness—man honors the spirits involved so that his actions may be concerted with and enhanced by theirs. He seeks to understand their will and fits his to theirs through appropriate ceremonies and rituals, usually involving the sacrifice of a lesser being. Since life is the supreme value, the taking of a life (usually goats, chickens, or cattle) opens communication with the source of life. (This theme is one found in almost all major religions, Western and Eastern.) The taking of a human life, the most important of all, is a sacrifice of a desperate people, for all other sacrifices have failed them in the search for answers to their problems. In actuality, human sacrifices have been rare in Africa, though novelists would have us believe otherwise.

Chapter 11

WHY PEOPLE HAVE DIFFERENT PREFERENCES:

FAMILY AND POPULATION

Each person tends to believe that his or her own particular perceptions are not personal but universal. What makes sense to oneself also seems to be just "common sense." As Americans, we hold such common-sense assumptions about many aspects of our culture, especially those that are so much a part of our everyday lives that we take them for granted. In this chapter, we will look at the American family and at how our perceptions of it influence how we perceive world population growth.

The family is a social unit that is found in every culture, and it exists in many varieties. Each culture, not surprisingly, tends not only to favor its own family system but also to consider it superior to and more humane than others. For example, some American textbooks refer to India's system of arranged marriages in the following judgmental way: "Indian children are rushed into marriage at an early age by anxious parents who pay an unreasonable dowry." Let us examine some aspects of this statement within a cultural context.

In many cultures today, people believe that marriage should take place when the bride and groom are biologically ready to have children. Few Americans know, however, that this belief was held by people in the United States from colonial times until the early nineteenth century. During this period, the fertility rate of women approached its highest level—about 55 births per 1,000 population.

In India—especially in its villages, where 70 percent of its people live—girls are reared with the expectation that they will one day marry; upwards of 98 percent (as compared to about 80 percent in the United States) eventually do. The marriages are arranged by family elders—a system that to most Indians, including those to be married, makes more sense than the "chance" matings that are customary in the West. After the Indian couple are married, the bride almost always moves into the husband's house, where his parents, his brothers and their wives and children, and any unmarried siblings also live. This arrangement is called, appropriately, the joint-family system. The emphasis is on group welfare. The bride's main contribution to the joint family is to provide children—especially sons, who will help ensure the family's survival and continuity. Ask a villager to name the most unfortunate among his or her neighbors, and the villager likely will point to a childless household, regardless of its income or landholdings.

Until recently, Indian villagers knew that the odds were only about fifty-fifty that a child would survive to adulthood, mainly because the death rate in the first year of life was as high as four out of ten. The death rate among infants is now less than two out of ten. The birthrate, however, has declined at a much slower rate. Rapid population growth has resulted.

To suggest to the villagers that their lives might be easier if their families were smaller is to ask them to risk their future. They are understandably uncertain and cautious because they fear having no one to look after them when they are sick and old. As a Hindu proverb concisely states: "You have a future when your grandson plays at your door."

Today in the United States, people have come to assume that the size of one's family should be determined by one's "ability to pay for it." In our culture, from the viewpoint of economics, children are seen more as a financial liability than as an asset. Most Americans have chosen to have fewer children as a result of this outlook. The current national birthrate (about 15.5 births per 1,000 persons) is among the lowest in our history. Dependence on grown children for help and support in old age has been replaced, increasingly, by pensions, personal savings, Senior Citizen communities, and government programs such as Social Security and Medicare. In fact, increasing numbers of Americans are deciding not to have children at all because the cost of rearing a child makes their preferred standard of living—including automobiles, appliances, travel, modern housing, recreation, and the like—less affordable.

PERCEPTIONS OF FAMILY AND POPULATION

Many Americans believe that their contemporary outlook on the family and on population growth follows common sense. Because of this "common-sense" perspective, they believe that people of other cultures who are generally poorer than Americans—namely Asians, Latin Americans, and Africans—would want to have smaller families or, perhaps, no children at all. In these places, however, the reality is that children continue to be regarded as economic assets. Before people in Asian, Latin American, and African cultures can be expected to limit the size of their families, other conditions must develop that will provide them with economic security. Americans tend to argue for a reduction in birthrate as a first step to well-being; those whom we are trying to persuade tend to resist taking this step until conditions change in their lives. In our own country, lower birthrates came about only after technological advances allowed family members to provide more surely for their own economic security.

These differing views on marriage, family, and economic security influence how people perceive population growth. Many Americans, for example, perceive the increase in world population as a problem created by non-Americans. We do admit to population problems in the United States when they occur among low-income families. Years ago, however, when production depended more on labor and less on machines, population growth among the poor was welcome. It was also welcome when armies depended more on manpower. In rural areas especially, children were an asset to the family because they could help with the work. In cities, older children and young adults could earn cash and share it with their families.

Historically, the American family has, in many ways, functioned like the family in India, encouraging strong feelings of usefulness, security, solidarity, and affection. To this day, the family in most cultures remains the center of existence. Ceremonies associated with births, initiations, weddings, and deaths are very much family affairs.

The pattern of American family life began to change dramatically during World War II when large numbers of women, for the first time, began to work outside the home in response to wartime employment needs and opportunities. After the war ended in 1945, many women continued to be employed. Today, four out of five married women are in the work force, and women as a group make up about 40 percent of the total number of employed Americans. The average American family now consists of 3.2 persons, in contrast to about 7 persons in 1800. Today, about 25 percent of America's households have only one person, and nearly one in six American children grow up in households where only one parent is present.

The issue here is not family and population; it is about making assumptions. By examining our own assumptions and resulting preferences, we can begin to understand how the peoples of other cultures arrive at their preferences. This awareness will help keep us from thinking that their ways are wrong. We should not urge a course of action on another cultural group without having at least some knowledge of and empathy for that group's culture and preferences.

CULTURAL VALUES AND
POPULATION PRESSURES

The question of family size is only one reason for our population pressures. The term *population pressure* is usually defined as "an increasing number of people who are competing for limited resources." This definition may have been appropriate once, but today in industrialized countries not only people, but goods as well compete: machines, packaging, sports goods, appliances, power stations, highways, and the like—all of which require raw materials. The ability of the world to support a growing population is affected by an even greater problem: the insistent demand for new and more products and services. This demand comes especially from countries that have a high standard of living—those that include less than 15 percent of the world's population but that consume more than 75 percent of the world's resources.

The demand for resources is related to cultural values as well as to ability to pay. For example, a newspaper advertisement advocating birth control showed a picture of an infant and was titled "We Can't Lick the Environmental Problems Without Considering This Little Fellow." The ad listed in some detail the enormous amounts of goods that the growing child "would scream for over the next seventy years." However, the ad did not raise the equally important question, how much of this demand is culturally induced?

While we are urging other people in the world to act "responsibly" in facing the "population crisis," we point with pride to the dynamic growth of our economy, which promises to consume goods and services at an even greater rate. When the *facts* of resource use are reported, the conclusions that follow are made according to preconceived patterns of perception. A newspaper article, for example, warns that the world is running out of raw materials because they are being consumed at a rate sharply above the rate of population increase. Faced with this dilemma, one choice would be to encourage restraint in resource use. Instead, reflecting the views of a consumer-oriented culture, the article concludes: "The upgrading of other nations to our standard of living is a sure path to disaster unless checks in population can be achieved."

What is desirable depends ultimately upon what is valued. If people were valued more, then an increase in population would be considered good news. In the United States, the automobile population is now over 135 million—up from about 89 million in 1970—but this increase is not called an "automobile explosion"; it is called "valuable economic growth," and therefore almost no one has recommended that the automobile population be controlled.

A former United States Secretary of the Interior once suggested that Americans need "an ethic of national thrift. . . . We can combine conservation and technology to redefine progress—and produce life-styles that will be leaner and more fulfilling. In the words of Gandhi, our slogan should be: 'There can be enough for everybody's need, but not enough for everybody's greed.'"

An "ethic of national thrift" need not necessarily deprive people of resource use. Zen philosophy, for example, teaches the concept of "the living use of materials and goods." When one is brushing his or her teeth and leaves the water faucet on, the water flowing into the drain has no "living use." Likewise, there is no "living use" of electricity when a light is left on in a vacant room (unless it is left on for security reasons). The Zen approach is less concerned with whether one can financially afford to waste resources and more concerned with appreciation and respect for conserving resources.

Many Americans realize that the economic inequalities between poor people and rich people are growing, both abroad and at home. Often the suggested solution for poor people is that they reduce their numbers. However, the poor of the world are increasingly asking, what are the well-off prepared and willing to modify in the way in which they live?

According to Buckminster Fuller, internationally acclaimed architect and inventor: "We know scientifically that for the first time in history there can be enough to support continually all of expanding humanity . . . there *is* enough to go around." The problem, however, says Fuller, is that we have had a technological revolution but not a humanistic one. We will not have one until we restructure the patterns of our thinking. It is not enough just to add new facts. Our relationships with other peoples of the world will worsen if we persist in a single-minded view that assumes that "what is good for us is good for them." The ease with which one can take this position depends on one's own circumstances. The *Panchatantra,* India's ancient textbook for the wise conduct of life, says it well:

"Each one for himself, said the elephant
as he danced among the chickens."

Confucius when asked what he would do first
if he became the head of a government said:
"I would see to it that things are called by
their right names. For if things are not called
by their right names, then the statements
would be misleading and when the statements are
misleading, then nothing can be accomplished."

COMMUNICATING WITH EACH OTHER

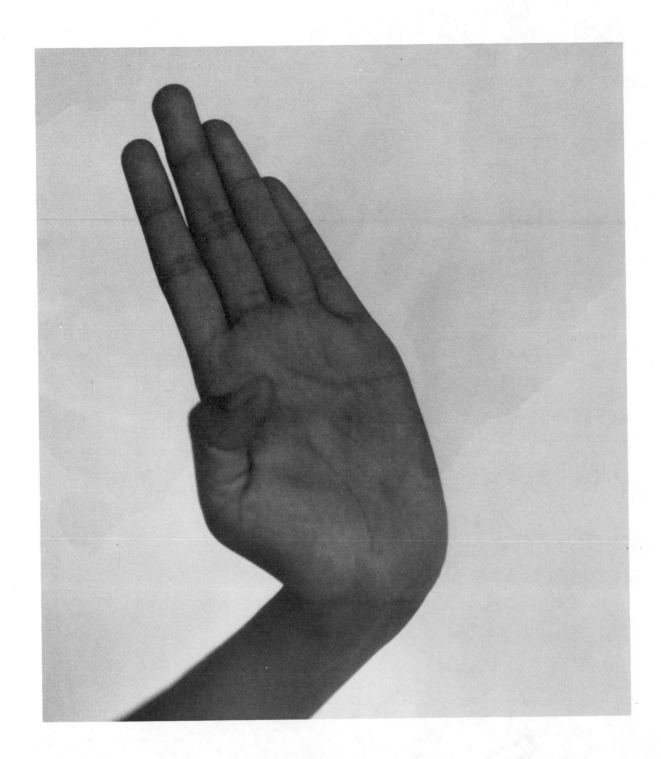

Chapter 12

MAKING SENSE WITHOUT WORDS

EDWARD
T. HALL, JR.

One role of the anthropologist is to prepare people to open their eyes and to sensitize them to the subtle qualities of behavior—tone of voice, gestures, space and time relationships—that so often build up feelings of frustration and hostility in people from a different culture. Whether we are going to live in a particular foreign country or travel in many, we need a frame of reference that will enable us to observe and learn the significance of differences in manners.

The anthropologist's job is not merely to call attention to obvious taboos or to coach people about types of thoughtless behavior that have very little to do with culture. One should not need an anthropologist to point out, for instance, that it is insulting to ask a foreigner: "How much is this in real money?" Where technical advice is most needed is in the interpretation of the unconscious aspects of a culture—the things people do automatically without being aware of the full implications of what they have done.

Nobody is continually aware of the quality of his own voice, the subtleties of stress and intonation that color the meaning of his words or the posture and distance he assumes in talking to another person. Yet all of these are taken as cues to the real nature of an utterance, regardless of what the words say. A simple illustration is the meaning in the tone of voice. In the United States we raise our voices not only when we are angry but also when we want to emphasize a point, when we are more than a certain distance from another person, when we are concluding a meeting, and so on. But to the Chinese, for instance, overloudness of the voice is most characteristically associated with anger and loss of self-control. Whenever we become really interested in something, they are apt to have the feeling we are angry, in spite of many years' experience with us. Very likely most of their interviews with us, however cordial, seem to end on a sour note when we exclaim heartily: "WELL, I'M CERTAINLY GLAD YOU DROPPED IN, MR. WONG."

The Latin Americans, who as a rule take business seriously, do not understand our mixing business with informality and recreation. We like to put our feet on the desk. If a stranger enters the office, we take our feet down. If it turns out that the stranger and we have a lot in common, up go the feet again— a clue to the other fellow that we feel at ease. If the office boy enters, the feet stay up. If the boss enters and our relationship with him is a little strained at the moment, they go down. To a Latin American this whole behavior is shocking. All he sees in it is insult or just plain rudeness.

In Latin America, where touching is more common and the basic units of space seem to be smaller, the wide automobiles made in the United States pose problems. People don't know where to sit. North Americans are disturbed by how close the Latin Americans stand when they converse. "Why do they have to get so close when they talk to you?" "They're so pushy." "I don't know what it is, but it's something in the way they stand next to you." And so on. The Latin Americans, for their part, complain that people in the United States are distant and cold—*retraidos* (withdrawing and uncommunicative).

An analysis of the handling of space during conversations shows the following: A male brought up in the northeastern United States stands 18 to 20 inches away when talking face to face to a man he does not know very well; talking to a woman under similar circumstances, he increases the distance about 4 inches. Reducing the distance between males is considered aggressive. Yet in many parts of Latin America and the Middle East, distances which would seem almost sexual in connotation to a North American are the only ones at which people seem able to talk comfortably. In Cuba, for instance, there is nothing suggestive in a man's talking to an educated woman at a distance of 13 inches. If you are a Latin American, talking to a North American at the distances he insists on maintaining is like trying to talk across a room.

To get a more vivid idea of this problem of comfortable distance, try starting a conversation with a person 8 to 10 feet away or one separated from you by a wide obstruction in a store or other public place. Any person can't help trying to close up the space, even to the extent of climbing over benches or walking around tables to arrive within comfortable distance. United States businessmen working in Latin America try to prevent people from getting uncomfortably close by barricading themselves behind desks, typewriters, or the like, but their Latin American office visitors will often climb up on desks or over chairs and put up with loss of dignity in order to establish a special context in which interaction can take place for them.

The interesting thing is that neither party is specifically aware of what is wrong when the distance is not right. They merely have vague feelings of discomfort or anxiety. As the Latin American approaches and the North American backs away, both parties take offense without knowing why. When a North

American, having had the problem pointed out to him, permits the Latin American to get close enough, he will immediately notice that the latter seems much more at ease.

The embarrassment about intimacy in space applies also to the matter of addressing people by name, but finding the proper distance in the use of names is even more difficult, because the rules for first-naming are unbelievably complex. As a rule we tend to stay on the ''mister'' level too long with Latins and some others, but very often we swing into first-naming too quickly, which amounts to talking down to them. Whereas in the United States we use Mr. with the surname, in Latin America the first and last names are used and señor (Sr.) is a title. Thus when one says, ''My name is Sr. So-and-So,'' it is interpreted to mean, ''I am the Honorable, his Excellency So-and-So.'' It is no wonder that when we stand away, barricade ourselves behind our desks (usually a reflection of status) and call ourselves mister, our friends to the south wonder about our so-called good neighbor policy and think of us as either high-hat or unbelievably rude. Fortunately most North Americans learn some of these things after living in Latin America for a while, but the aversion to being touched and to touching sometimes persists after 15 or more years of residence and even under such conditions as intermarriage.

The difference in sense of time is another thing of which we are not aware. An Iranian, for instance, is not taught that it is rude to be late in the same way that we are. In a general way, we are conscious of this, but we fail to realize that their time system is structured differently from ours. The different cultures simply place different values on the time units.

Thus let us take as a typical case the time system in the urban eastern United States. A middle class businessman meeting another of equivalent rank will ordinarily be aware of being two minutes early or late. If he is three minutes late, it will be noted as significant but usually neither will say anything. If four minutes late, he will mutter something by way of apology. If five minutes late, he will utter a full sentence of apology. In other words, the major unit is a five-minute block. Fifteen minutes is the smallest significant period for all sorts of arrangements, and it is used very commonly. A half hour, of course, is very significant, and if you spend three quarters of an hour or an hour, either the business you transact or the relationship must be important. Normally it is an insult to keep a public figure or a person of significantly higher status than yourself waiting even two or three minutes, though the person of higher position can keep you waiting or even break an appointment.

Now, among urban Arabs in the eastern Mediterranean—to take an illustrative case of another time system—the unit that corresponds to our five-minute period is 15 minutes. Thus when an Arab arrives nearly 30 minutes after the set time, by his reckoning he isn't even ''ten minutes'' late yet (in our time units).

Stated differently, the Arab's tardiness will not amount to one significant period (fifteen minutes in our system). An American normally will wait no longer than thirty minutes (two significant periods) for another person to turn up in the middle of the day. Thereby he often unwittingly insults people in the Middle East who want to be his friend.

Informal units of time such as "just a minute," "a while," "later," "a long time," "a spell," "a long, long time," "years" and so on are not as imprecise as they seem. Any American who has worked in an office with someone else for six months can usually tell within five minutes when the person will be back if he says, "I'll be gone for a while." It is simply a matter of learning from experience the individual's system of time indicators. . . . Spelled out, the message might go somewhat as follows: "I am going downtown to see So-and-So about the Such-and-Such contract, but I don't know the traffic conditions or how long it will take me to get a place to park nor do I know what shape So-and-So will be in today, but taking all this into account I think I will be out of the office about an hour but don't like to commit myself, so if anyone calls you can say I'm not sure how long I will be; in any event I expect to be back before 4 o'clock."

Few of us realize how much we rely on built-in patterns to interpret messages of this sort. An Iranian friend of mine who came to live in the United States was hurt and puzzled for the first few years. The new friends he met and liked would say on parting: "Well, I'll see you later." He mournfully complained: "I kept expecting to see them, but the 'later' never came." Strangely enough, we ourselves are exasperated when a Mexican can't tell us precisely what he means when he uses the expression *mañana.*

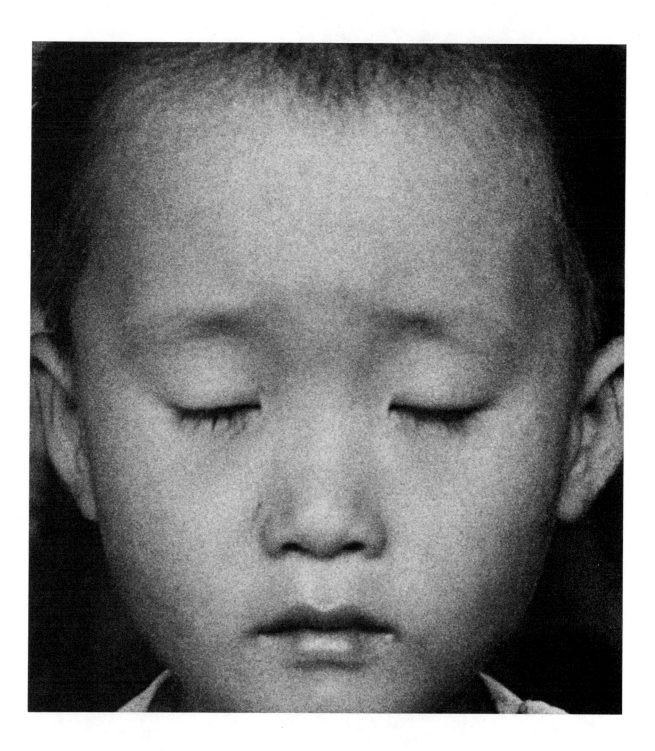

Chapter 13

THE IMPORTANCE OF LANGUAGE IN COMMUNICATION:

A JAPANESE VIEWPOINT

**MASAO
KUNIHIRO**

I firmly believe that one major reason for "discommunication" between Japan and the United States lies in the great dissimilarity between the two countries in nonverbal communication or mental attitudes, notwithstanding the close surface similarity in terms of economy, technology, systems, institutions, and so forth.

First of all, it is absolutely essential that our American friends understand that in our culture, language itself, or communication through language, has not had the same importance it has had in the West. Instead of being a means of conveying one's own will or thoughts, language has merely been, so to speak, a way of casually throwing the other guy a ball in order to get a reaction from him on which to base one's next action. It has been considered poor policy to use language to express one's views, persuade the other guy, and establish mutual understanding. Using language for debates, the purpose of which is to "agree to disagree" as is done by English-speaking peoples, has been considered even more disagreeable and has been avoided accordingly.

Let me give you a couple of examples of "casually throwing the other guy a ball." Take the case of a person saying, "I've already eaten," when he drops in at a friend's house at mealtime. If his friend takes him at his word and doesn't try to persuade him to have something to eat anyway, he stands a good chance of being criticized later for being insensitive or unconcerned about others. One is supposed to make sure that he wasn't just being polite by saying something like "Ah, come on. Join us anyway" or "You're not just being polite, are you?" In this way language becomes a sort of ritual. One might say that in Japanese society it isn't often taken at face value. What we have come up with to compensate for such distrust of language is nonverbal communication. Come to think of it, Japanese is rich in sayings such as "eyes speak as much as words" and "far better than to say something is not to say it." . . . The Japanese expression *i-shin-den-shin,* "the heart is conveyed by the heart," is an indication of the height of nonverbal communication. Thus, in Japan language is *a* means of communication, not *the* means of communication as it often is in the case of English.

Contempt for or distrust of language can also be seen in the attitude of Japanese companies toward contracts in spite of the fact that they ought to be one of the most modern elements in Japanese society. It is still quite common for contracts between even large manufacturers and large trading firms not to be in writing. One might even go so far as to say that contracts exist only for the purpose of specifying stipulations that are an exception to the rule. Actually, I have been told by an expert in such matters that in the overwhelming number of cases, an escape clause which reads something like "all other problems will be settled through consultation" is included in written contracts between even large corporations.

What, then, are the reasons behind such distrust of or contempt for language? Also, what makes possible the kind of Japanese "community of emotion" in which words are very sparingly used, at least when expressing feelings? Why is there a preference for expressions that can only be described as vague, the expectation being that the other guy will be concerned enough to grasp one's meaning correctly? In answer to these questions I would like to make the following points, which I hope will be of use to our American friends.

First of all, we have to consider Japan's unparalleled homogeneity. Japan is an island country surrounded by seas on four sides, and there have been few, if any, countries in the world where a single ethnic group has lived for such a long time using the same language throughout its history.

With such a high degree of natural unity and singleness, the degree of mutual understanding among the members of the society, too, is extremely high. This is because, first of all, they share the same life-style and attitudes. In other words, very much the same kind of logic has wide currency in society in general and in communication within the family. Although the Japanese, both as individuals and as a group, are adept at close communication, they are extremely handicapped when it comes to distant communication. . . . For instance, two strangers—even if they are both Japanese—sitting next to one another in the train will exchange hardly any conversation to speak of, with the result that the atmosphere between them is cold and strained. And when the communication is with different racial and ethnic groups, with which of course there is no feeling of familiarity whatsoever, the unpleasantness is doubled.

The second reason that should be noted for the Japanese contempt for language and, therefore, for their sparing use of words is the highly hierarchical structure of Japanese society. In this hierarchy the will of those farther up the ladder is conveyed on down, but it is taboo for someone on a lower rung to give free and uninhibited expression to his opinions. In Japan the family principle of vertical society acts as the bond in human relations, exerting a frightful degree of compulsion on the individual members of society. . . . In modern Japan, the most highly industrialized society in Asia, the dynamic tendency to hold together the social fabric vertically by this family principle displays a remarkable tenacity in almost all areas of modern life. . . . [Our] development of techniques of non-verbal communication [takes] the form of "reading the minds of one's superiors from their facial expressions" and "guessing what they are thinking." In other words, we understand international relations in terms of the same superior-subordinate relations, the same relations of vertical society, and base our actions on this understanding.

Now I would like to discuss the question of what has happened as a result of the special nature of the Japanese attitude toward language.

First let me say something about what might be called the aesthetics of silence, or the way of thinking that makes a virtue of reticence and a vulgarity of open expression of one's inner thoughts. A good example of this way of thinking is the expression *fu-ryu-mon-ji,* or "words are of no use," in Zen Buddhist philosophy, which had its beginnings in China and matured in Japan. The idea here is a kind of metaphysics that sees man as capable of arriving at the highest value only when he makes no attempt at verbalization and discounts talking or anything that can be expressed in words as being the height of super-ficiality. The aesthetics of silence does not necessarily indicate that the Japanese are not easily moved. Far from it. What exists there is a desire to depend on others,[taking] it for granted that the other guy will understand, as well as a sincere regard for his feelings.

Consider the discrepancy between the English word *sincerity* and the Japanese word *seijitsu* roughly in the following way. According to anthropologist Ruth Benedict the meaning at the root of the English word *sincere* or *sincerity* is the frank expression of one's inner thought without mincing words and without considering what effect one's words will have on the person who is listening. On the other hand, she says, if a Japanese were to behave in a like manner, he would probably be accused of insincerity. Being a foreigner, I'm not in a position to pass judgment on the nuance of the English word, but as far as the Japanese words go, I think what she says here is basically right. If it is, not only does the dictionary equalization of the words *sincerity* and *seijitsu* have the rug pulled out from under it, but the bizarre equalization of *sincerity* and *fuseijitsu* (insincerity) becomes justified. Actually, the fact that words in the two languages which according to the dictionary ought to be equivalent are often not equivalent is a major problem point in U.S.-Japanese communications, and bridging the gap here is going to be an unglamorous job that will have to be started at as early a date as possible. Leaving this problem aside for the moment, I would, however, like to stress the necessity for our American friends to realize that we Japanese feel hesitant to give frank and definitive expression to our inner thoughts—we even feel a sort of social restraint working here.

Nevertheless one would be out of touch with reality if he were to say that this sort of consideration is shown only to avoid hurting the other guy's feelings. Another motive is the strong fear that by opening up one's heart with full candor, that is, "sincerely," as one would say in English, one might become isolated from the group to which one belongs. In the homogeneous society of the Japan of former days with its large population and scarcity of resources, limited opportunity for employment, and no possibility at all for fleeing abroad, such isolation would have been equivalent to committing suicide.

A disturbing attitude is that of the mother of a celebrated commentator who

gave her son the following advice: "No matter what you do, don't take the lead. When all the others stage a strike, you shouldn't be the only one who doesn't participate, for that could lose you your place in the group. But in any case the worst thing you could do is to take the lead." To her the most important thing was to pay as much attention as possible to the adjustment of relations with others so as to prevent quarreling with others in one's group and not to be thought ill of by either superiors or subordinates. And this is something that has to be taken note of equally by all Japanese of every walk of life even today.

Chapter 14

SEMANTICS AND THE STUDY OF CULTURES

Consider such words as *poverty, underdeveloped, hot, cold, democratic, progressive, backward,* and the like. Dictionaries carry definitions, but people carry connotations—and it is connotations that influence thinking and rule behavior.

Throughout history, many writers in many cultures have called attention to the fact that words misinform as well as inform, but it was not until 1897 that a Frenchman, Michel Breal, created the term "semantique," or the science of meaning. More recently, in the 1920s in the United States, a movement called General Semantics was pioneered by Alfred Korzybski and subsequently popularized by researchers and writers, including Stuart Chase, Wendell Johnson, S. I. Hayakawa and Irving Lee. Borrowing ideas from these and other writers on the subject, we have drawn a number of examples to illustrate the contribution an understanding of semantics can make to any study of other people and other ways of life.

SOME ASSUMPTIONS

The nature of the world is one of dynamic flow—"a mad dance of electrons"—in which no two things are identical, no one thing remains the same and, as Heraclitus expressed it over 2,000 years ago, "one cannot step in the same river twice."

The nature of humans is that—unlike other living things—we can "receive gifts from the dead" through the use of language, but our internal experiences are literally "unspeakable"—that is, they defy description. Abstractions take place when we try to substitute words for reality.

The nature of language is like that of a map; it is useful to the extent that it describes the territory accurately. Maps and territories are not the same, however, nor are words and reality interchangeable.

SOME APPLICATIONS

1   **No two things are identical.**

For example, South American 1 is not South American 2 is not South American 3 is not South American 4. In other words, a South American teacher in Lima is not a South American rural worker in Brazil. Although by agreement we refer to the 275 million people who live in an area called South America as South Americans, the truth is that no two South Americans are identical—including, of course, those who live in the same country or even in the same household. Considered in the same way, each of the estimated 85 billion people who have inhabited the earth has been unique.

Statements which seem to talk about "a people" as if they were one entity must obviously be qualified. Questions such as "What do Africans think about Europeans?" are clearly unanswerable. Answerable questions—those which have some likelihood of being verified—are less dramatic and perhaps less satisfying, but that is the nature of the problem. It is only by taking liberties with language that we appear to be better informed than the data permit. Similarly, it may readily be seen that terms such as "African," "Oriental," "Muslim," and the like conceal differences as well as reveal group likeness.

2   **No one thing stays the same.**

Japan of 1840 is not Japan of 1945 is not Japan of 1985 is not Japan of 2000, and so forth. Change is inevitable, though the rate varies. One who forgets this is certain to be shocked when confronted with the difference between what he thinks (or remembers) is true and what is so.

3   **It is not possible to tell all about anything.**

No matter how complete a listing or how comprehensive an explanation, the possibility always remains open that something more might be said about the matter under consideration. All descriptions are "open-ended" with the last word unsaid. Completeness may be a goal, but like infinity it eludes mortal grasp. Thus, for example, an examination of any culture or any country might include reference to its history, its development, its achievements, and so on, but these would always be incomplete. No matter how extensive the treatment, a mental "etc." should be added to the last punctuation point. The practical effect of this orientation is to leave the door open, at least a crack, for additional information which may be forthcoming.

4   The same word may be used to represent different "realities," while similar events or experiences are sometimes called by different names.

For example, a term such as *republic* is used to designate two very different political systems—that of the United States and that of the Peoples Republic of China. A boisterous mass of people might be called a "mob" by a person opposed to the group and a "party" by someone who enjoyed being with the group. Other words, such as *radical, conservative, liberal,* and *reactionary,* often are used as labels. Words such as these whose meanings have become meaningless from being used to carry too heavy and too diversified loads of information should be set apart by enclosing them with quotation marks to alert the reader. Korzybski used to wiggle two fingers of each hand to achieve the same effect when speaking.

5   Statements of opinion are often confused with statements of fact.

For example, verb forms of *to be* often cloud the relationship between subject and predicate, as when someone says, "It is hot." The "hotness" is more a description of the speaker's state of mind than it is of the temperature reading, since what constitutes "hot" is a matter of opinion. "Cold wave" could mean anything from 20 or 30 degrees below zero (F.) in the Himalayas to 40 degrees above in New Delhi where, incidentally, a continuous string of days in the 90s in May would scarcely qualify as a "heat wave." Very often, the addition by the speaker of the words "to me" and the addition by the listener of the words "to you" helps to identify so-called statements of fact as opinions.

**SOME
SUGGESTIONS**

1   Try to use descriptive terms rather than ones which express approval or disapproval.

For example, the words *clean* and *unclean* are relative. The comment that cow dung is used for fuel in many Indian villages often provokes reactions of disgust from many urban dwellers in the United States. It may be instructive on this point to quote from a Kansas editor, writing in 1879 at a time when buffalo and cow dung (he calls them "chips") were commonly used for fuel: "It was comical to see how gingerly our wives handled these chips at first. They commenced by picking them up between two sticks, or with a poker. Soon they used a rag, and then a corner of their apron. Finally, growing hardened, a washing after handling them was sufficient. And now? Now it is out of the bread, into the chips and back again—and not even a dust of the hands."

2   **Try to use phrases that indicate conditions which should be considered with a statement.**

For example, awareness may be increased by the use of such phrases as "in our culture," "from our point of view," and "at that time."

3   **Try to move in the direction of substituting precise words for vague ones.**

For example, it is often said that "heavy rains" fall on India during the monsoon season. The statement would carry more meaning if it were pointed out, for instance, that Allahabad, a city in the Ganges Valley, and New York City both receive an average of forty inches of rain annually *with* the significant difference that New York City gets from two to four inches of precipitation monthly whereas Allahabad is hit by some thirty-seven inches within the months of June to October. The description of rainfall in "annual" amounts makes sense only when the downfall comes in relatively equal inches per month.

4   **Try to become more alert to the ways in which cultural conditioning shapes our value judgments.**

For example, historian Carroll Quigley reports:

> We divide the whole range of colors, as found in the rainbow, into six colors: red, orange, yellow, green, blue, violet. With our background, we think a view is beautiful if it consists of alternating horizontal bands of green and blue, as in a landscape consisting of a foreground strip of green shore, a blue lake beyond, a farther shore of green trees and hills, and a blue sky beyond that.
> But to a Bantu of dry Africa, such a view is a rather boring panorama of a single color, for many natives of that language-group place green and blue in a single category with one name, although they divide the lower red-orange-yellow portion of the spectrum into a larger number of basic colors, with names. That is why what impresses us as a beautiful view of shore, lake, and sky strikes them as a rather monotonous field of one color, whereas, conversely, an African view, which to us seems to be a dull expanse of semiparched soil with dry grasses, may seem to them to be an exciting scene of many different colors.

5   **Try to recognize the degree to which the mind itself projects the kinds of answers which it obtains.**

For example, writer Carl Sandburg tells of the responses which newcomers to Kansas received from one of the local farmers:

"What kind of folks live around here?" "Well, stranger, what kind of folks was there in the country you come from?" "Well, they was mostly a low-down, lying, thieving, gossiping, backbiting lot of people." "Well, I guess, stranger, that's about the kind of folks you'll find around here." And the dusty gray stranger had just about blended into the dusty gray cottonwoods in a clump on the horizon when another newcomer drove up: "What kind of folks live around here?" "Well, stranger, what kind of folks was there in the country you come from?" "Well, they was mostly a decent, hardworking, lawabiding, friendly lot of people." "Well, I guess, stranger, that's about the kind of folks you'll find around here."

6 **Try to avoid either-or evaluations, substituting instead the idea of a continuum which encourages answers expressed by "in-between" amounts when appropriate.**

For example, in our culture we often ask questions about the weather, such as: "Do you think it will snow?" The form of the question seems to suggest that it will or it won't; either yes or no. But to Eskimos, for example, "snow" is described by about 50 different names, each one indicating a degree of snow varying from blizzard-size to snowflakes. Each kind of snow is important in knowing what the "road conditions" for dog-sleds will be. Similarly, skiers have developed many new names to describe conditions on the slopes.

7 **Try to become more suspicious of our own "wisdom."**

Anatole France once said of a man, "He flattered himself on being a man without prejudices; and this pretention itself is a very great prejudice." In *The Devil's Advocate: A Plea for Superstition,* written in 1909, Sir James G. Frazer argued that so-called superstitions more often than not embody a realistic distillation of experience whereby the uninitiated and unwary may receive tested guidance. Behind many "myths" are "truths" which have helped people to rationalize and maintain social order and organization. Thus, for example, the "superstition" held widely in many Asian countries that the left hand is "evil" or in some ways inferior to the right hand becomes more acceptable to the Westerner when he becomes familiar with the functions for which the left hand is reserved exclusively—functions which he would readily agree were "unclean" and worthy of giving the left hand its "bad reputation."

SOME IMPLICATIONS

Of course, much of what has been pointed out will not necessarily come as a startling revelation. None of the ideas are new, and many under different names, have been used by intelligent people who have never heard the word "semantics,'' let alone been exposed to the writings of Korzybski and others. So much the better! Our concern is not so much with *how* people distinguish between a ''map'' and the physical territory that it describes, but that they *do* distinguish. George Orwell writes, ''What is above all needed is to let the meaning choose the word, and not the other way about. . . . Probably it is better to put off using words as long as possible and get one's meaning as clear as one can through pictures and sensations.''

No one is suggesting that all abstractions be distrusted. ''In demanding that people cease reacting to abstract names as if they were realities in themselves,'' says S. I. Hayakawa, ''we are merely saying in another way, 'Stop acting like suckers.' '' And until we do give more disciplined attention to words, we will continue to stockpile symbols and labels while the ''precious commodities''

which are being symbolized and labeled escape our detection and comprehension. The argument-ending remark, "It is *only* a matter of semantics," must give way to the significant recognition that the "real" search for "meaning" may very well start where words leave off.

When someone is seeking, it happens quite easily that he only sees the thing that he is seeking; that he is unable to find anything, unable to absorb anything, because he is only thinking of the thing he is seeking, because he has a goal, because he is obsessed with his goal. Seeking means: to have a goal; but finding means: to be free, to be receptive, to have no goal. You, O worthy one, are perhaps indeed a seeker, for in striving towards your goal, you do not see many things that are under your nose.

Herman Hesse

Chapter 15

CULTURAL DIFFERENCES WITHIN A COUNTRY:

DIVERSITY WITHIN UNITY

Our awareness of cultural differences among people who live in different countries can help us understand and appreciate differences among groups within a country. Such awareness is especially helpful in the United States, because ours is a nation where 99 percent of the population are immigrants or descendants of immigrants who came here within the past four hundred years. What we have learned about foreign cultures can be applied to learning about Americans of foreign ancestry. Writing in 1855, the American poet Walt Whitman celebrated the United States as "not merely a nation but a teeming nation of nations."

THE AMERICAN
ETHNIC HERITAGE

The United States Census Bureau uses the nation of origin as its way of identifying a person's ethnic group. The most recent census statistics show that out of a total population of about 250 million, English and German ethnic groups number about 50 million each. Other groups with more than 10 million are: Irish, 40 million; African-Americans, 30 million; French, 13 million; Italian, 12 million; and Scottish, 10 million. Those who identified themselves as American Indians number 1.4 million, and the Hispanic group (mainly from Mexico, the Caribbean area, and Central America) number about 18 million.

To understand the changes regarding the place and perception of ethnic groups in the United States, it is useful to focus on a particular group. Let us, for example, consider the history of the Asian-American immigrant experience in the United States. A Chinese saying states that where there is a horse and cart, there are really three things: a horse, a cart, and a horse-and-cart. This wise observation recognizes that people and events together produce results that are dynamic and interrelated as well as interacting and highly unpredictable.

THE ASIAN-AMERICAN
IMMIGRANT EXPERIENCE

A good place to start is with the word *Asia,* which is from the Greek word for "sunrise." To the Greeks, China and Japan were the lands of the rising sun. Likewise, the Latin word *oriens,* meaning "east" led to the designation of the "Eastern" part of the globe as the Orient. Consequently, people who live in the Orient are sometimes called "Orientals." The English verb *orient* provides another clue: It means "to adjust with relation to surrounding circumstances; to *orient* one's ideas to new conditions." If one faces the rising sun, one can become better oriented to other directions.

As a name for a racial category, however, the term *Oriental* conceals more than it reveals. Just as the word *European* is inadequate to identify Italians, French, Germans, Swedes, and English, the term *Oriental* fails to identify the various peoples of Asia. In fact, the term *Oriental* has often been used to stereotype all people whose ancestry is Asian. This definition denies each of the Asian nationalities the right to be appreciated as a separate ethnic group.

In the 1980 census the total number of Asian Americans in the United States amounted to nearly 4 million. Of this number, the three largest groups are the Chinese (about 900,000), the Filipinos (about 800,000), and the Japanese (about 800,000). The next largest groups are the Koreans (about 400,000), the Asian Indians (about 350,000), and the Vietnamese (about 250,000).

Let us now consider the history of the three Asian-American groups that immigrated primarily before World War II: the Chinese, the Japanese, and the Filipinos.

ASIAN AMERICANS IN
HISTORICAL PERSPECTIVE

Most American history textbooks have presented Asian Americans (called Orientals until after World War II) in an unrealistic way or hardly mentioned them at all. This is unfortunate. Americans should know about the treatment Asian Americans have received in the United States.

The Chinese were the first to come. Their labor was welcomed in the gold rush of the 1850s in California. Later their numbers increased rapidly when many hands were needed to complete the transcontinental railroad. By 1870, there were about 65,000 Chinese in the United States. Only a few hundred were women because the Chinese, except for diplomats and merchants, were not allowed to bring women or wives to the United States. In the next ten years, 250,000 more Chinese came. About 80 percent lived in California. To the impoverished Chinese worker, America was a bountiful land, and its name in the Chinese language meant "rice country."

American attitudes toward the Chinese changed when immigrants of European ancestry reached the West Coast and competed for jobs. At first the Chinese were considered orderly, industrious, thrifty, sober, and inoffensive. By the 1880s they were seen—in the minds of most civic and industrial leaders—as clannish, secretive, dangerous, criminal, and deceitful. The Chinese themselves had not changed; the change was in the mind of the viewer, not the viewed.

The growing discrimination against the Chinese led to the Chinese Exclusion Act of 1882, which denied immigration for ten years to Chinese laborers. The act was renewed in 1892, and Chinese immigration was suspended indefinitely in 1902. During this time, many Chinese returned home. The Exclusion Act also denied citizenship to Chinese who were not born in the United States, a discriminatory measure which later affected other Asians and continued until shortly after World War II. About 250,000 Chinese lived in the United States in 1882, but the number decreased to 90,000 in 1900 and to 60,000 in 1920. The Chinese who remained suffered from discrimination and legal abuse.

Japanese immigration to the United States occurred almost entirely within the first quarter of this century, ending in 1924 when the Asian Exclusion Act provided for the total exclusion of all "aliens ineligible for citizenship." Discrimination against the Japanese followed the same pattern of prejudice encountered by other "yellow men," even though the Japanese tended to follow the European immigration pattern—bringing their wives and eventually settling in integrated communities. The United States government, in the "Gentlemen's Agreement" of 1908, persuaded the Japanese government to restrict the immigration of Japanese laborers and farmers to the United States so that friendship between the two countries would not be disrupted.

Drastic discrimination against the Japanese came during World War II, when, by presidential decree, the total Japanese population of more than 120,000 people in Oregon, Washington, and California (of whom two-thirds were United States citizens and one-third were resident aliens ineligible for citizenship) was evacuated to ten "relocation centers" in remote places in the western United States. Most evacuees remained in camp until the end of the war. The communities were hastily constructed barracks, enclosed by barbed wire and kept under armed guard. The relatively small Japanese populations in other parts of the United States were widespread and were not forcibly relocated. Hawaii, home to about 100,000 Japanese-Americans, was required to turn over only its most influential leaders for internment. To relocate all of Hawaii's Japanese-Americans (about a quarter of the total population) would have severely damaged the islands' capacity to function, and adequate shipping would not have been available because of other priority wartime demands.

Most Filipino Americans came to Hawaii and California in the 1920s. Like other Asians, they were ineligible for naturalization, but because the United States governed the Philippines as a colony, the Filipinos carried United States passports and could not be excluded as aliens. In 1932, the United States pledged that it would grant the Philippines independence within fifteen years and then proceeded to enforce an immigration quota of fifty Filipinos annually. Thus ended any significant immigration of Asians into the United States until after World War II.

ASIAN AMERICANS TODAY

Since World War II, attitudes and actions towards Asian Americans have been changing. In 1943, in recognition of the American wartime alliance with China, the Chinese Exclusion Act was repealed. In 1952, the Asian Exclusion Act of 1924 was repealed, and race was eliminated as a barrier to becoming a naturalized United States citizen. In 1965, Congress repealed the national origin quota system as the basic United States immigration law. The earlier immigration law of 1924 discriminated especially against Asians because it limited the number of immigrants from a country to a total based on the percentages of foreign-born persons of the same nationality who already were living in the United States at the time of the 1890, and later 1920, census.

In 1986, the immigration law was changed again. It now provides that the total number of immigrants may not exceed 270,000 annually and that no more than 20,000 may come from any one country.

The 1965 repeal of the national origin quota law greatly changed the percentages allowed in each group; it also allowed immigration to the United States to increase by about one-third. For example, from 1900 to 1965, about 75 percent of immigrants were Europeans. Since 1965, about 75 percent have been Asians and Latin Americans. Asian-American immigration increased from 20,000 in 1965 to about 130,000 in 1975.

In the decade of 1970–1980, the Asian-American population increased by about 150 percent: the Chinese and Filipino groups almost doubled, and the Japanese increased by about a fourth. For the first time, large numbers came from Korea as well as from South Asia and Southeast Asia. The current Asian-American population represents about 1.5 percent of the total United States population, double its 1970 percentage.

Most Asian Americans in the United States live in urban areas. More than three-fourths of them reside in seven states: California, Hawaii, New York, Illinois, Texas, Washington, and New Jersey. The largest number, about 1.5 million, live in California, where they represent about 5.5 percent of the population; the next largest number, about 600,000, live in Hawaii, where they represent about 60 percent of the population.

The changes in the immigration laws after World War II also were accompanied by other attitudinal changes. Specifically, in 1976 President Gerald Ford recognized the injustice that the Japanese-Americans had suffered. In a proclamation he said:

"In this Bicentennial Year, we are commemorating . . . many great events in American history. An honest reckoning, however, must include a recognition of our national mistakes. . . . We now know what we should have known then—not only was the evacuation wrong, but Japanese-Americans were and are loyal Americans. . . . I call upon the American people to affirm this American promise—forever to treasure liberty and justice for each individual American, and resolve that this kind of action shall never again be repeated."

In 1988, the Congress overwhelmingly approved and President Ronald Reagan signed legislation which authorized an apology for the loss of freedom to the Japanese-Americans who had been interned and a payment of $20,000 to each internee to compensate for loss of property.

CHANGING PERCEPTIONS OF OUR ETHNIC HERITAGE

When the first United States public schools were established in the 1830s, their major goal was to help create students who were loyal Americans with a single standard of behavior. This Americanization process—a "melting pot" where many ethnic ingredients would be blended to produce one nationality—was considered necessary for a nation of immigrants. From the start, the English language and Western European culture were the major ingredients of the melting pot; minority ethnic groups added seasoning but were to be absorbed.

Now there is growing support for multi-ethnic education in American schools. More Americans believe that our culture should include greater respect for differences in racial, religious, and ethnic heritage. We are trying to create and sustain a nation that recognizes more truly our special nature as a land of immigrant ancestry.

One of our problems has been in perceiving American ethnic groups as a "problem." We often have failed to appreciate—literally, "to add value to"—the enrichment and stimulation our ethnic differences have contributed to an American culture. When we begin to welcome ethnic variations as an opportunity rather than as a problem, the realities of American life can be experienced more fully. The former mayor of Newark, Kenneth Gibson, expressed this view eloquently when he said he hoped the United States would become a "nation of racial, ethnic, and religious diversity, a mosaic of pluralism where each knows and honors his own roots and can, therefore, be secure enough to honor what is different in his neighbor."

Chapter 16

CHANGING PATTERNS OF PERCEIVING

We are not surprised that there are cultural differences among the peoples of the world because we all live in different places—different geographic areas. Nor are we surprised that there are cultural differences within a country such as the United States. After all, our immigrants brought their cultural habits and attitudes with them, and while conditions in the "New World" modified many of these cultural preferences, most immigrants retained some of their ethnic heritage.

Today, there are other kinds of "New Worlds" that are affecting cultural changes, worlds which exist more in technology than in geography. In the past century, the speed of human travel has increased by 100 times, the power of energy by 1,000 times, the power of weapons by 1 million times, and the speed of communication by 10 million times. More importantly, perhaps, the nature of change itself is changing; there is more of it, and its rate has accelerated.

Unlike earlier conditions, the new ones are mainly of our own making; we can congratulate or blame ourselves for our present situations. For most of human history the physical environment remained relatively unchanged, and people were able to use traditional methods and ideas that had time to mature slowly in harmony with technological changes. The future could be approached along paths that were mainly extensions of time-tested routes.

Now, however, humankind faces extinction unless we can learn to change our behavior *before* we create environments to which we will be unable to adjust. The degree to which technological innovations become blessings rather than burdens depends upon our "intelligent foresight of consequences," in John Dewey's words. We must become futurologists, consciously and actively determining in advance what kind of future we prefer.

This new necessity (and opportunity!) makes the study of human societies essential because we all belong to cultures and need to know more about how they are created and how they function. We need more information and more understanding, but more than these we need new methods of learning.

About fifty years ago, sociologist Robert Lynd wrote about a way of perceiving which he called "the outrageous hypothesis." What happens, he asked, if one examines a question by considering a hypothesis *opposite* the one which first comes to mind? Is it possible, after all, that what we consider to be a logical hypothesis is based more on our habitual way of thinking than it is on the facts themselves? Why, for example, do "fact-finding missions" usually return with facts that serve to prove the opinions and assumptions of the people who created them?

A similar suggestion for "outrageous thinking" comes from Edward de Bono, who says that "Until today ideas have always lived longer than people, but now people live longer than ideas. As a result there is great need for mental tools that make possible re-forming of ideas." He calls his method "zigzag thinking" —a mixture of *vertical thinking* (ideas based on experience) and *lateral thinking* (ideas based on imagination). An important ingredient in zigzag thinking is humor, because the mixture of ideas often provides a sudden reversal in the ways a situation can be perceived. As the "punch line" of a joke succeeds if it is not anticipated, so zigzag thinking often reveals insights that yield only to unpredictable patterns of finding.

Chapter 17

THE VIRTUES OF ZIGZAG THINKING

**EDWARD
DE BONO**

When you can't solve a problem with a frontal attack,
try detours and reversals.

Our whole culture is concerned with establishing concepts
and communicating them—but not with changing them.
I know of no facet of education that examines the technique of changing or updating ideas. The tacit assumption
is that it is enough to generate information and that
eventually the pressure of information will bring about a
change in concepts. This is the basis of the scientific
method. But the pressure of information is an insufficient
process. Experiments are designed and the results interpreted in the light of the old concepts, which tends to
preserve the old concepts far longer than the information
warrants.

"FOGWEED" CONCEPTS

It often happens that some unplanned intrusion of information is required to bring about a restructuring of a
concept. Once this is done, everyone is agreed that there
was enough evidence to suggest it long ago. This concept
lag may be very long. In spite of these disadvantages, the
scientific method is moderately efficient. But outside the

technological field, progress has been extraordinarily slow. Where new evidence *can* only be interpreted through the old concept, the old concept is strengthened, no matter what the evidence. One easily gets a myth situation—a myth being any idea which controls the possibility of conflicting evidence.

There are fields in which progress has been held up for ages because of the dominance of obstructive mythlike concepts. A convenient term for such concepts is "fogweed," because they grow readily on fertile soil, and quickly obscure. Furthermore, enriching the soil with more information only strengthens the fogweed.

VERTICAL THINKING

You cannot dig a hole in a different place by digging the same hole deeper—and vertical thinking is digging the same hole deeper. You start from what you have and go straight ahead, using any one of the many effective information-handling techniques available. Vertical thinking is the highly esteemed (and rightly so) traditional method of thinking that has proved immensely effective, especially in technological matters. It has three basic characteristics:

1 **Vertical thinking is a stepwise process.** Each step follows on from the previous step in an unbroken sequence.

2 **Vertical thinking must be correct at every step.** (This is perhaps the very essence of the process.)

3 **Vertical thinking selects and deals only with what is relevant.**

LATERAL THINKING

What is lateral thinking? Instead of digging the same hole deeper, lateral thinking digs a hole in a different place. As the name implies, lateral thinking is thinking sideways: not developing a pattern but restructuring a pattern.

The use of information in the two types of thinking is fundamentally different. In vertical thinking, information is used for its own sake, as a contribution to the development of a structure. In lateral thinking information is used provocatively in order to bring about a restructuring.

Lateral thinking therefore contradicts all three of the characteristics of vertical thinking:

1 **Lateral thinking is not sequential.** One may make a single jump or a series of jumps to different entry points. The common practice of tackling a problem from the solution end rather than the starting end is an example of this process. Instead of constructing a pathway by inching forward, one jumps to different points and then allows the fragments between to coalesce.

2 **Lateral thinking does not have to be correct at each stage.** Since information is being used provocatively and in a catalytic manner, one may be wrong or ridiculous in order to snap the pattern into a new alignment that makes sense. The end justifies the means. Judgment is suspended. It may be necessary to pass through a "wrong" area in order to reach a position from which the correct path may be visible. It may be necessary to be wrong within a frame of reference in order to update that frame of reference.

3 **Lateral thinking is not restricted to relevant information.** On the contrary, lateral thinking deliberately uses random or irrelevant information to bring about a perturbation of the system—something that cannot happen from within itself.

REVERSING DIRECTION

One simple lateral technique is reversal. Wherever there is a direction, the opposite direction is implied. (Asked to redesign the human body, a seven-year-old child asked for eyes that could use "black" light.) Reversal simply means taking the obvious idea and turning it inside out, upside down, back to front. . . .

In an Eastern country there was an heiress whose father wanted her to marry the richest of her many suitors, but she herself was in love with a poor student. Being a lateral thinker she tried "reversal" and said to herself: "Supposing Daddy was actually to pay this poor student to marry me." So she went to her father and told him that she wanted to be sure of marrying the richest of her suitors. The father was delighted. The daughter then asked him how they were going to tell which man was the richest of her suitors. It would be no use asking them to put on a display or present a gift, for they would easily be able to borrow money if the daughter's fortune was to be gained by so doing.

"Let us do the opposite," she said. "Let us give each of them a large sum of money and then we can tell how rich each of them is by the difference this present makes in his way of life—and to prove this is so we must give the same sum to the student whom we know to be poor." The father congratulated the daughter on her subtlety and gave out the sums of money. Whereupon the daughter eloped with the now enriched student.

This reversal technique illustrates the basic nature of the lateral process. Its purpose is not so much to find an answer . . . but to provoke a new unstable structuring of the situation and then let it develop. It is rather like siphoning water out of a container. One sucks the water upward in an unnatural direction and then lets it flow.

Chapter 18

CULTURAL DIFFERENCES WITHIN A CULTURE:

WOMEN AND THE LANGUAGE OF INEQUALITY

**ELIZABETH BURR,
SUSAN DUNN,
NORMA FARQUHAR**

A language is not merely a means of communication; it is also an expression of basic assumptions. When basic assumptions change, the words or phrases that express them become obsolete. Following are some suggested changes in language designed to eliminate expressions that reflect outdated assumptions concerning women.

MASCULINE TERMS THAT INCLUDE FEMALES

Masculine terms are commonly believed to include or refer to females as well as males. In fact, however, such terms operate to exclude females. When told that "*Men* by the thousands headed west" or that "The average citizen of the United States is proud of *his* heritage," the young reader simply does not form a mental image which includes females. It is of no avail for a parent or teacher to explain that *men* means *both men and women,* or that *he* means *both he and she.* Even an adult is unlikely to picture a group of amicable females when reading about "men of good will." Similarly, when taught that *man*-made improvements have raised America's standard of living, or that a task requires a certain amount of *man*power, a child cannot be expected to develop the concept that females as well as males have participated in the developmental process. . . .

NOBODY KNOWS
HER NAME

Reflecting a time when females were in fact the possessions first of their fathers and then of their husbands, who were empowered by law to beat them, sell them, or otherwise dispose of them arbitrarily, girls and women are still referred to primarily in the obsolete terms of those who "own" them. In textbooks, females are typically referred to merely as *wives* (Mrs.), *daughters* (Miss), or *mothers of* males, who are clearly identified by name and occupation. Such possessive terms of reference deliver the implicit message that in and of themselves females are of no particular interest or importance and reflect the assumption that marital status is the crucial fact of life for women.

Compare, for example, the following two sentences: (1) George Ferris married the daughter of the wealthy Boston banker, Edward Howell. (2) Alice Howell of Boston, heir to a banking fortune, married George Ferris. The second sentence recognizes Alice as a person in her own right; the first, in which she is *nameless,* suggests that whatever shadowy identity she may have possessed depended upon the identity first of her father and then of her husband. Similarly, phrases such as "the farmer's wife" clearly convey the idea that the female was merely a possession of the farmer and was not herself a farmer, when in fact the wives of most small farmers were themselves farmers *in every sense of the word.*

MALE-ORIENTED QUOTED
MATERIALS

[Authors' italics.] (1) "*Men* since the beginning of time have sought peace. . . ." (General Douglas MacArthur); (2) "The American is a new *man,* who acts upon new principles; *he* must therefore entertain new ideas, and form new opinions . . ." (J. Hector St. John de Crèvecoeur); (3) "These are the times that try *men's* souls." (Thomas Paine); (4) "The New Englander, whether *boy* or *man,* in a long struggle with a stingy or hostile universe, had learned also to love the pleasure of hating; *his* joys were few." (Henry Adams). The above and similar quotations which are to be found in textbooks reflect the opinion that females are of no consequence. Such quotations are permissible in textbooks only as examples of contemporary prejudiced attitudes toward women.

Some documentary material, however, will inevitably be regarded as necessary in a textbook in spite of the fact that it is couched in male-oriented language. A case in point is the Gettysburg Address: "Fourscore and seven years ago our *fathers* brought forth on this continent a new nation, conceived in liberty, and dedicated to the proposition that all *men* are created equal. . . . and that government of the *people,* by the *people,* for the *people,* shall not perish from the earth." If this or similar male-oriented documents are quoted, the textbook should point out the male orientation of the language. Any textbook quoting the Gettysburg Address should, for instance, indicate that when President Lincoln spoke of *people* he had in mind *males,* because at the time of his famous speech, females were not permitted to vote and were denied many legal rights enjoyed by men.

NEUTRAL OCCUPATIONAL TERMINOLOGY

Occupational terms ending in *man*—such as airman, fireman, cameraman, anchorman, statesman, workman, iceman, repairman, watchman and salesman—are objectionable because they suggest that certain fields of endeavor are closed to women. Premodern terms such as bondman or plowman, used in a discussion of pre-modern times, may be permissible, but modern sex-affiliated terms should be eliminated. They not only give young people false impressions about their future vocational prospects; they also tend to perpetuate discriminatory practices that do indeed exist.

People who do not want to use or invent new terminology can evade the issue by recasting entire sentences. For example, "Mr. Jones sent for a TV repairman" can be revised to "Mr. Jones called a TV repair service." The ending -*man* is, however, increasingly being replaced by -person to form terms like "chairperson." The word "salesperson" is already accepted, and other neutral terms will gain acceptance as the decisive influence of language on the attitudes and lives of people becomes more widely understood.

TERMS TO BE AVOIDED

"Just a *housewife*" is a frequently heard expression, the nature of which is indisputable. It conveys the derogatory attitude of society toward the woman who works as a homemaker and the consequent self-contempt which she feels. The term *housewife,* moreover, clearly suggests that domestic chores are the exclusive burden of females. It gives female students the idea that they were born to keep house and teaches male students that they are automatically entitled to laundry, cooking, and housecleaning services from women in their families. The inculcation of such attitudes is inconsistent with the ideal of equal educational and vocational opportunities. The term *housewife* should therefore never be used.

Similarly, where men are referred to as *men* rather than *husbands,* but women are referred to as *wives* rather than *women,* the textbook is again treating men as *persons, not husbands,* and women as *wives, not persons.* The term *wife* should therefore be used only sparingly.

The following terms and expressions should be regarded as demeaning and should not be used: *lady* (as synonym for adult female), *girl* (as synonym for adult female), *the little woman, the weaker sex,* and *squaw.*

Such terms as *author, aviator, heir, laundry worker, sculptor, singer, poet, Jew,* and *Negro* are neuter terms which are *without exception* properly applicable to both females and males. The use of words ending in "feminine" suffixes, such as *authoress, aviatrix, heiress, laundress, sculptress, songstress, poetess, Jewess,* and *Negress* is unacceptable. Terms ending in "feminine" suffixes imply that females are a special and unequal form of the correct neuter expression. Thus, to speak of Edna St. Vincent Millay as a *poetess* is to exclude her from the legitimate circle of *poets;* to speak of Amelia Earhart as an *aviatrix* denies her full status as a *aviator;* to speak of Golda Meir as a *Jewess* denies her full status as a *Jew,* and so on. In cases where it is necessary to indicate the sex of the individual, the expression "female poet," "female aviator," "female Jew" and so on may be used. However, in modifying neuter terms the word "lady" (as in "lady lawyer," "lady doctor," "lady poet," and so on) is never acceptable.

Chapter 19

HUMANKIND: NEW CONDITIONS, NEW OPPORTUNITIES

Albert Schweitzer observed: "The difference between white and black, between civilized and primitive, disappears when one talks to the inhabitants of the primeval forest about questions concerning our relations with ourselves, with other peoples, with the world and with eternity."

If, as human beings, we are more alike than we are different, then why through recent tens of centuries have we rarely recognized and emphasized these similarities? Evolution in cultural forms, as well as in biology, is rarely accidental. Our present forms of life — physical and social — are mainly a response to specific conditions. To understand why we identify by group rather than by species, we need to understand how we became the way we are.

For about 100,000 years *homo sapiens* was only one of many species competing for survival. The general conditions from the start were competitive — kill or be killed, feed upon or be fed upon. But earliest people certainly saw themselves as being related when compared to other species. Their first actions were to cooperate with each other for their own survival against non-human threats — from nature and from animals.

About 13,000 b.c., there began perhaps the most significant series of events in human history—agriculture started to replace hunting as the major means by which people secured their livelihood. Humans settled down not only in a physical sense; they also began to establish patterns of life and thought which still dominate our assumptions about survival. Life based on agriculture was relatively fixed. Those who possessed fertile lands survived better than those who did not. War was clearly beneficial to the victors when it resulted in gaining better lands and additional workers in the form of slaves. Warfare was not pleasant, but it was usually profitable for the winners.

Asking people always to be peaceful was asking them to act against their own self-interest and survival. Those who had property, it was assumed, would always be envied, feared or threatened by those who did not. The world was seen as being divided into "the haves" and "the have nots." For protection, groups of people—families, clans, nations, allies—organized themselves against other groups. It became part of cultural wisdom that one's own security and prosperity could be achieved only at the expense of other groups; hence, one must be prepared for the eventual attempts at invasion or reprisal. Individuals who did not belong to protective groups were likely to be the victims of those who did.

**THE NEW BALANCE
OF BENEFITS**

In considering whether our past actions are still appropriate for the future, we should not assume that people were acting unintelligently before. They may not have been. The conditions were different; their actions may have been relatively appropriate to their situation. But what are the conditions now?

In recent centuries, people's lives have been significantly affected by two major inventions: mechanical energy is replacing human and animal energy, and computers are duplicating and sometimes surpassing some of our thought processes. People can now gain more from cooperation than from conflict. Consider the possibilities now open to humankind through the cooperative application of technology. Transoceanic telephone messages, for example, which used to require hundreds of thousands of tons of copper cable, are now being sent via laser beam over fiber-optic cables that are thinner than a child's wrist. Moreover, the new equipment transmits thousands more calls simultaneously and at a higher level of fidelity than before. For years peoples and nations have believed that resources were limited and aggressively safeguarded their portions. Now, new technology allows more efficient use of resources thus lessening the need for conflict.

**THE CHANGING CONDITIONS
OF CHANGE**

It is now essential that new assessments of our situation be made in advance of experiencing them. Just as physical scientists are trying to devise ways of detecting evidence of approaching earthquakes, we must try to anticipate the implications of new human conditions.

To change our perspectives is not as difficult as it may first seem. The ways in which we view the world, other people and ourselves is, after all, the result of education, formal and informal. Humans are not born with conceptions; we learn them. We need not feel helpless once we have identified the problem area. We can gain encouragement and direction from what Professor Kenneth Boulding has written:

In this case we can put the problem in the form of a change in the "nuosphere," to use a concept of Pierre Teilhard de Chardin's. The nuosphere is the total body of knowledge as it exists in the five billion minds of the human race spread over the surface of the earth. The existing nuosphere is almost certainly not consistent with human survival in the long run, or even in the next few decades. We believe too many things which are not true, we do not know things that are true, and we have values (which are also as part of nuosphere) which are inconsistent with the successful management of conflict or the process of human development. We should not, however, relapse into pessimism on this account, because the nuosphere is capable of change and even of rapid change.

Today, more people throughout the world are trying to understand each other but a willingness is not enough. It takes careful attention and concern. It is, for example, often said that we live in a shrinking world—a world which has become a neighborhood. And this is true when distance is measured by the time it takes to transport a person or to transmit a message. There is, however, another kind of distance—the "space" which separates the minds of people. And measured in this way, Americans are *farther* away than ever from their world neighbors.

Despite rapid urbanization since 1900, more than half the world's people live in villages, many without electricity and running water. Increasingly, Americans live in cultural contexts which have widened the way-we-live-distances between ourselves and others—especially those who live in Asia and Africa. The greatest need for us, then, is not merely to increase the intake of facts but to become alert to our own special outlook towards those who live differently.

Never before have we had the opportunity to know so much about the world we inhabit—its peoples, its natural resources, its technological potential. But it is also true that the quality of life, and respect for the individual worth of each person may be lessening. We need to reaffirm that the proper study of humankind is still humans. What Comenius, over two hundred years ago, implored us to do has now become an imperative:

We are all citizens of one world, we are all of one blood. To hate a man because he was born in another country, because he speaks a different language, or because he takes a different view on this subject or that, is a great folly. Desist, I implore you, for we are all equally human. . . . Let us have but one end in view, the welfare of humanity.

ACKNOWLEDGMENTS

The African-American Institute: For "African Mythology" from *Are You Going To Teach About Africa?* by Susan Hall. American Anthropological Association and Professor Horace M. Miner: For material from "Body Ritual Among the Nacirema" by Professor Horace M. Miner, from the *American Anthropologist.* Elizabeth Burr, Susan Dunn and Norma Farquhar: For "Women and the Language of Inequality" by Elizabeth Burr, Susan Dunn and Norma Farquhar from *Social Education,* December 1972. W.H. Freeman and Company Publishers: For material from "The Anthropology of Manners" by Edward T. Hall, Jr. from *Scientific American,* April 1955; copyright © 1955 by Scientific American, Inc. Professor Raymond Gorden: For "Cross Cultural Encounter in a Latin American Bank" by Raymond Gorden. Indiana State University, School of Education: For material from "Education in a World of Nations" from *Contemporary Education;* this material appears in the selection "Humankind," at the end of this text. International Business Machines Corporation: For "The Virtues of Zigzag Thinking" by Edward de Bono from *Think* Magazine, May-June 1969, published by IBM; copyright 1969 by International Business Machines Corporation. Macmillan Publishing Company, Inc.: For "How Attitudes Are Sometimes Formed" by Philip Foster from *Africa South of the Sahara.* For material from *Latin America* by Harold Peterson, in The Culture Regions of the World series, edited by Seymour H. Fersh. National Council for the Social Studies: For material from "Studying Other Cultures: Looking Outward Is 'In' " by Seymour H. Fersh, from the 1968 *Yearbook.* Phi Delta Kappa: For material from "Orientals and Orientation" by Seymour H. Fersh from the *Phi Delta Kappan,* January 1972; copyright 1972 by Phi Delta Kappa, Inc. Patricia Hughes Ponzi: For material from "The Sacred 'Rac' " by Patricia Hughes Ponzi; copyright 1973 by Patricia Hughes Ponzi. Allen Raymond, Inc.: For material from "Viewpoint" in article entitled "Semantics and the Study of Cultures" by Seymour H. Fersh, from *Early Years* Magazine, 1973. *Topic* Magazine: For material from "The Liberal Values of Non-Western Studies" by Yu-Kuang Chu from *Topic,* a Journal of the Liberal Arts, published by Washington and Jefferson College, Washington, Pennsylvania, Spring 1962. The authors and editors have made every effort to trace the ownership of all copyrighted selections found in this book and to make full acknowledgment for their use.

ILLUSTRATIONS

Michael Hoffman, 7, 25, 115; The Bettmann Archive, 14, 18; University of Chicago, 23 (top); Black Star, 24; Magnum, 30, 39, 40, 50, 55, 59, 66, 80, 85, 94-95; Museum of Primitive Art, 47, 56, 65; Woodfin Camp & Associates, 58, 72-73; The Oakland Museum 74, 79, 96; Rapho-Guillumette, 102; The Cleveland Museum of Art, 106-107, 109; TWS-Click/Chicago, 60.